around NEW YORK CITY with KIDS

by Mindy Bailin

4th EDITION
FODOR'S TRAVEL PUBLICATIONS
New York * Toronto * London * Sydney * Auckland

www.fodors.com

Credits
Writer: Mindy Bailin

Editor: Paul Eisenberg
Editorial Production: Evangelos Vasilakis
Production/Manufacturing: Angela L. McLean

Design: Fabrizio La Rocca, *creative director;*
Tigist Getachew, *senior art director*
Cover Art and Design: Jessie Hartland
Flip Art and Illustration: Rico Lins, Keren Ora Admoni/
Rico Lins Studio

About the Writer
New Yorker Mindy Bailin is a teacher and mother of three who writes about family, education, and health. She is the Director of Bet Torah Nursery School in Mt. Kisco, New York.

Fodor's Around New York City with Kids

Fourth Edition
ISBN 978-1-4000-1929-8
ISSN 1526-1468

An Important Tip and an Invitation
Although all prices, opening times, and other details in this book are based on information supplied to us at press time, changes occur all the time in the travel world, and Fodor's cannot accept responsibility for facts that become outdated or for inadvertent errors or omissions. So always confirm information when it matters, especially if you're making a detour to visit a specific place. Your experiences—positive and negative—matter to us. If we have missed or misstated something, please write to us. We follow up on all suggestions. Contact the Around New York City with Kids editor at editors@fodors.com or c/o Fodor's at 1745 Broadway, New York, New York 10019.

Special Sales
This book is available for special discounts for bulk purchases for sales promotions or premiums. Special editions, including personalized covers, excerpts of existing books, and corporate imprints, can be created in large quantities for special needs. For more information, write to Special Markets/Premium Sales, 1745 Broadway, MD 6-2, New York, New York 10019, or e-mail specialmarkets@randomhouse.com.

PRINTED IN THE UNITED STATES OF AMERICA
10 9 8 7 6 5 4 3 2 1

COUNTDOWN TO GOOD TIMES

GET READY, GET SET!

Go ahead. Take a bite of the Big Apple and count down to fun while you visit the 68 places that appear in this handy-dandy collection of favorite places and spaces to explore. Whether you're day tripping in the city, planning a weekend family getaway, or spending a weeklong vacation here, there's no better place to be than N-Y-C (or the entire metropolitan area surrounding the city, if you really want to know). These 68 great things to do together include sites in Manhattan, as well as Brooklyn, the Bronx, Queens, and Staten Island. A few sights in New Jersey and Westchester and on Long Island are also included. They're only a stone's throw from the Big Apple and worth the trip.

LOOK INSIDE

Each two-page spread in this book describes a great place to take your family. The "toolbar" at the top of the page lists all the particulars: address, phone numbers, admission prices, hours, and age recommendations. **Make the Most of Your Time** boxes offer practical information that will help you maximize your experiences; **Eats for Kids** identifies family-friendly restaurants near the sights; and **Keep in Mind** presents factoids and tips that both you and children will appreciate.

Also in the toolbar are Web addresses for most attractions. Some sites offer virtual tours of these great destinations, which may get your family in the mood for a "field trip." Many Web sites also include learning activities, background information on exhibits, and calendars of events, classes, and programs open to the public. It's worth a look before you plan your visit, and after you go, these Web sites can be great resources for kids who want to learn more.

To get started, just flip through the book, keeping an eye peeled for the Statue of Liberty's magical transformation. It could only happen in New York. You can find places of interest to your family by just leafing through the listings (in alphabetical order) or by looking in the directories in the back of the book. "All Around Town" groups sights by neighborhood, helpful if you're planning to visit more than one attraction or are looking for additional kid-friendly dining choices. (Call ahead for travel directions and parking availability.) "Something for Everyone" groups attractions by type, such as parks and gardens or free attractions.

BE PREPARED
The prices listed in the book are regular adult, student (with ID), and kids' prices (children under the ages specified are free), but there are often ways to get a bargain. When planning your visit, always check local newspapers and family publications for coupons, special discounts, and combination tickets. Many attractions also offer discounts if you belong to an automobile club or other designated organizations. Some places even offer free admission on certain days or at certain times. When in doubt, check it out.

Call ahead to confirm prices, discounts, and hours of operation. The hours listed in this book are an attraction's basic hours, not necessarily those applicable on holidays. Also inquire about the busiest times for these attractions. When school is in session or during summer camp, lines can be long and crowds may be unbearable. On those days, consider a late-afternoon visit, after the groups have headed for the buses.

Don't forget the sunscreen and hats for sunny days and outdoor locations, pocket ponchos or folding umbrellas for rain, and the portable stroller or backpack for walking distances with very young children. Be sure to pack water bottles or juice drinks to quench your thirst and a few snacks to hold the group over before your lunch or munch break. Do be mindful of those attractions that prohibit food or drink in exhibit halls or other spaces. Most importantly, remember this book. It easily slips into a diaper bag, beach bag, camera case, picnic tote, or purse. Don't leave home without it!

Pace yourself and your family during these excursions. There's no need to see every exhibit in the museum or every animal in the zoo. Focus on a few fun aspects of each attraction. Don't rush. If you have time for further exploration, go for it! But don't expect to cover the entire attraction in your first visit. Plan to come back, especially if this trip is a successful one for your young tourists. Please note the Intrepid Sea Air Space Museum is closed for renovation until fall 2008.

It goes without saying that you should keep a close eye on your children at all times, especially if they're small. To make sure your outing is safe and successful, consider dressing your children in bright, colorful, or same-color shirts or hats. It's not a bad idea for you to do the same, so your children can spot you in a crowd. Pick a visible landmark and a meeting time to reunite just in case you become separated. When you first arrive at your destination, identify staff and security people so everyone knows whom to ask for help or directions if needed.

MAKE IT LAST

The places included and the information provided was carefully chosen to help your family create "teachable moments" and lasting memories for your children. Finding something of interest for everyone is always a challenge, but most of these places appeal to a wide age range—from toddlers to teens, parents to grandparents. To create a "teachable moment" and make a memory last a lifetime, give your child a disposable camera to capture favorite experiences on film. After your excursion, make a family adventure scrapbook or photo album. Older children may want to create a video complete with kid commentary. Handwritten journals or computer-generated diaries are also creative and fun ways to record your family fun, and these family records tend to become priceless.

Did somebody say gift shop? Yes, most of the attractions in this book have some type of retail gift boutique on the premises. To avoid a severe case of the "gimmies," save this stop for right before you go home. Before entering those portals of pricey paraphernalia, agree on the amount of the purchase and hold firm. While a small and charming souvenir can immortalize the day, there's no need to break the bank.

DON'T FORGET TO WRITE

Is there a special attraction in our countdown that your family especially enjoys? Did we overlook one of your favorite places? We'd love to hear from you. Send your e-mails to me c/o editors@fodors.com. Please include "Around New York City with Kids" in the subject line. Or drop me a line by snail mail c/o Around New York City with Kids, Fodor's Travel Publications, 1745 Broadway, New York, NY 10019.

Wherever you go and whatever you do, have a great day. Remember you're exploring the greatest city in the world and you're traveling with the greatest kids in the world . . . yours.

Mindy Bailin

AMERICAN FOLK ART MUSEUM

There's something about folk art that appeals to children. Perhaps it's the seeming simplicity, the depictions of everyday objects and creatures, or the frequent flights of whimsy. But whatever the reason, your children will probably enjoy this collection.

The permanent collection highlights America's folk art heritage through paintings, sculpture, furniture, textiles, and decorative arts. Items of particular interest to kids include dolls, carousel horses, weather vanes, and whirligigs. *Uncle Sam Riding a Bicycle,* a sculpture that moves in the wind, and the colorful Flag Quilt, by Mary Baxter, are just two examples of the patriotic art preserved here. The fantastic scroll-like paintings of self-taught 20th-century artist Henry Darger are also part of the permanent display.

Children will enjoy *Girl in Red Dress with Cat and Dog* as they imagine how a young girl of the 18th century managed to pose for her portrait in her best red dress with a cat on her lap and a dog at her feet. Young visitors will also be intrigued by Santa Fe artist Felipe Archuleta's large painted wood *Tiger* carving with big red teeth, red tongue, real whiskers

MAKE THE MOST OF YOUR TIME Ask for the new family guide at the front desk, *Hello Folks.* It contains a colorful sheet for each floor of the museum filled with fun activities. The theme for the mezzanine is History's Mysteries, floor 5 revolves around Home Sweet Home, and floor 4 encourages Materials Madness. Also check out the Museum Shop for some cool books, games, and toys for children. Admission is free for all on Friday 5:30–7:30. Friday from 5:30 onward also features live music in the atrium.

45 W. 53rd St.

 $9 ages 12 and up

 T–Th and Sa–Su 10:30–5:30,
F 10:30–7:30

212/265–1040;
www.folkartmuseum.org

2 and up,
art workshop 5 and up

and painted toenails. The famous *Peaceable Kingdom* painted in 1846 by Quaker artist Edward Hicks will be most recognizable to middle-schoolers and high school students who will spot the animals, including the lion and tiger lying down peacefully together.

Folk Art Revealed, part of the permanent collection, includes the whimsical whirligig of a Witch on a Broomstick and the towering architectural Empire State Building, made without any nails or glue.

Guided tours, workshops, puppet shows, concerts, and storytelling take place year-round. Sunday afternoon art workshops, called Folk Art Fun for Families (reservations required), follow guided family tours of the museum.

If you like this site you may also like the New-York Historical Society (#22).

KEEP IN MIND Each year this museum, along with the Museum of Modern Art and the Museum of Arts and Design (40 W. 53rd St., tel. 212/956–3535) hold a "Shop the Block" event with a special day of shopping at all three retail stores, offering a 20% discount to museum members.

EATS FOR KIDS
The mezzanine level of the main museum features a small coffee bar. For a frightfully fun meal, try Jekyll & Hyde (1409 6th Ave., tel. 212/541–9505).

AMERICAN MUSEUM OF NATURAL HISTORY

67

This museum, a wonderful place of exploration, discovery, and learning for generations of children, contains more than 30 million specimens and cultural artifacts. Your youngest visitors will be excited and delighted to spend their time in the six spectacular halls containing the world's most comprehensive and scientifically important dinosaur collection. The five-story exhibit in the Theodore Roosevelt Rotunda, featuring a *Barosaurus* rising up to protect its baby from an *Allosaurus,* is the tallest freestanding dinosaur exhibit on earth. Also making children's and young teens' eyes sparkle is the Hall of Gems, which houses the Star of India, the world's largest and most famous blue star sapphire. The Spitzer Hall of Human Origins, which opened in 2007, presents the remarkable history of human evolution from our earliest ancestors millions of years ago to modern *Homo sapiens*. Exhibits explore where we came from, what makes us uniquely human, and what lies ahead for our species. Middle schoolers will find this new hall most interesting.

MAKE THE MOST OF YOUR TIME

The museum is huge, with 46 exhibition halls in 25 interconnected buildings. It's impossible to see the entire collection in one visit, so keep your focus narrow and plan to return often. Each year 4 million people visit, so no matter when you come, you won't be alone.

The Rose Center for Earth and Space, a monumental 120-foot-high, 333,500-square-foot exhibition, research, and education facility, houses the renovated Hayden

EATS FOR KIDS The **Museum Food Court** offers a wide variety of food for all ages and palates: stone-oven pizza alongside sushi, pasta, a salad and antipasto bar, grilled sandwiches, and smoothies. The **Café on 4** overlooks the grounds at 77th Street from a windowed turret. Bistro selections include light entrées, salads, desserts, and beverages. **Café on 1,** next to the newly renovated Grand Gallery at the 77th Street entrance, also offers gourmet sandwiches, tasty salads, and cold and hot drinks.

Central Park West at 79th St.

 212/769–5100, 212/769–5200 museum programs and tickets, 212/769–5993 natural science center; www.amnh.org

Suggested donation $15 ages 13 and up, $8.50 children 2–12; museum and space show $22 ages 13 and up, $13 children; IMAX extra

 Daily 10–5:45, space shows daily 10:30–4:30, 1st F of mth 10:30–7

2 and up

Planetarium, a must-see for all ages. A gleaming cube of glass envelops the magnificent Hayden Sphere, some 87 feet in diameter. The top part of the Hayden Sphere screens *Cosmic Collisions* narrated by Robert Redford, and the lower part screens *The Big Bang* narrated by Maya Angelou. Both are too lengthy for toddlers and young school friends, but both will capture the attention of the seven and up crowd. On Friday and Saturday evenings, *SonicVision,* a digitally animated alternative-music show with a mix by Moby, will captivate your teens. Though museum admission includes the Rose Center, the Hayden Planetarium Space Shows cost extra and advance tickets are advised.

If you tire of looking at exhibits, check the IMAX movie schedule for larger-than-life films that reveal nature's wonders, shown daily on a four-story screen.

If you like this sight you may also like the National Museum of the American Indian (#31).

KEEP IN MIND Ever piece together the skeleton of a prehistoric *Prestosuchus* (a 14-foot reptile from the late Triassic period)? If you haven't and you're up for exploring a hands-on "museum within the museum," then head to the renovated Discovery Room, an interactive gateway to the Museum's wonders. Here you and kids 5 and older can get up close and personal with some of the museum's collections. Older kids can analyze images from the Hubble Telescope and use a seismograph to track earthquakes worldwide, on the mezzanine level.

ASPHALT GREEN

It has Manhattan's only Olympic-standard pool that nonmembers can use on a pay-per-swim session basis, and that's saying something. The pool has been voted best in the city and residents rely heavily on its exceptional swim classes: parents and babies (starting at 4 months) can enjoy the warm-water moveable bottom pool for instructional swim.

The facility also has a regulation AstroTurf field for sports, two gyms, an indoor and outdoor running track, two outdoor parks, the Mazur Hall theater, and indoor and outdoor basketball courts. Add to that a duplex fitness center, aerobics rooms, gymnastics rooms, and a stunning rooftop deck. The facility also recently completed a multimillion-dollar renovation, which includes new locker rooms, lobbies, a private Pilates and yoga studio, a new café with wireless Internet access, and a new look throughout the building.

Established in 1968 where a former municipal asphalt plant once operated, Asphalt Green was created as a recreational center for city youth and the community at large. The

EATS FOR KIDS For healthy sandwiches, salads, and smoothies, not to mention kid-friendly snacks, visit Asphalt Green's new café. The gourmet soups are winners, too. **Eli's Vinegar Factory** (431 E. 91st St., tel. 212/628–9608), part of the Zabar's family of food stores, is open daily but has a restaurant component open only on Saturday and Sunday 8 AM–4:30 PM: Come for brunch, breakfast, lunch, or dinner for fabulous sandwiches, soups, salads, and pastas. For barbecued ribs, pork, and chicken and, not incidentally, a free kid's meal with the purchase of each adult entrée, it's hard to beat the generous and satisfying eating at **Brother Jimmy's Bait Shack** (1644 3rd Ave., tel. 212/426–2020).

parabolic plant building was declared a New York City landmark and today serves as a full-service sports and fitness complex. The city still owns the land, but in return for rental exemption, Asphalt Green provides a third of its services free to the community.

Children's classes are held in aquatics, sports and fitness, and martial arts. Offerings are varied and include swimming, diving, soccer, gymnastics, karate, and yoga. Private lessons are also available. Summer camp activities include sports and various arts: of the "fine," "performing," "crafts," and "martial" varieties. Holiday minicamps and sports clinics for 5- to 16-year-olds are held throughout the year and during school breaks. About the only thing you can't do here anymore is make asphalt.

If you like this sight you may also like Chelsea Piers (#55).

MAKE THE MOST OF YOUR TIME Each fall the Asphalt Games include clinics hosted by Olympians; kids under 3 can visit Toddler Village. In spring you can meet Olympic swimmers, earn a medal, and get cool free stuff at the annual Big Swim. Top swimmers in each event are invited to participate in an AquaShow, with some of the country's best swimmers, lights, music, and a cast of kids.

KEEP IN MIND
Going to the "green" portion of Asphalt Green, the complex contains Dekovats and Sundial Plaza parks, which have plenty of green space and gardens, park benches, and game tables. Dekovats adds a playground and a sprinkler in summer; Sundial Plaza has a fountain.

BROADWAY ON A BUDGET

65

With tickets for top shows costing more than $100 each, it can be expensive to give your family's regards to Broadway. Enter the Theatre Development Fund's (TDF) TKTS. At two locations—Duffy Square (Times Square) and South Street Seaport—you can purchase same-day discounted tickets to Broadway and Off-Broadway plays and musicals (though matinee tickets at the Seaport outpost are sold a day in advance). The names of available shows are posted by the outdoor booths. You probably won't get tickets to the season's smash hit—after all, they're only made available to TKTS if the theater isn't sold out—but there will undoubtedly be something that's entertaining.

Lines are shorter at the South Street Seaport location, but the wait on the often long line at Duffy Square usually moves fast, and if you get your tickets here, you'll be halfway there. You can kill time around Times Square, grab a bite, and walk to the theater. Remember to bring cash or traveler's checks, because TKTS doesn't take American Express—or other credit cards.

KEEP IN MIND If you're in doubt about which musicals or plays are family-friendly, avail yourself beforehand of the TDF Show Search (www.tdf.org) whose drop-down menu includes an "age guidance" option that sorts shows by age appropriateness.

EATS FOR KIDS For sports fans and those with a craving for a good ballpark frank, score a great lunch at the **ESPN Zone** (1472 Broadway, at 42nd St., tel. 212/921–3776). For home-style Italian pastas and chicken and veal dishes like mama used to make, served family style, you can't go wrong at **Carmine's** (200 W. 44th St., between Broadway and 8th Ave., tel. 212/221–3800). Choose from 17 burger toppings or split a gargantuan sandwich at the **Stage Deli** (834 7th Ave., tel. 212/245–7850). Don't forget the pickles. Also see NBC Studios Tour (#30), the New Victory Theater (#29), Radio City Music Hall (#12), and Rockefeller Center and the Ice Rink (#11).

TKTS, Duffy Sq., 47th St. and Broadway;
South Street Seaport, 199 Water St.

 Usually 50%–75% off
regular price plus $3
surcharge per ticket

Duffy Sq. M–Sa 3–8, plus W and
Sa 10–2, Su 11–7; Seaport M–Sa 11–6,
Su 11–4.

888/BROADWAY Broadway Line;
www.livebroadway.com,
www.kidsnightonbroadway.com

4 and up, but varies by
show

The Times Square location is most crowded when it opens, but around 5 PM there's usually no waiting in line for tickets for that evening's shows. To avoid a wait, however, go later in the day, but know that many of the day's offerings may be gone. In fall and nonholiday winter weeks, as many as 50 shows can be available, so don't despair. Family fare can usually be found. Though ticket sellers won't stop and chat they will tell you which shows have seats in the better locations. It's likely that your family can sit together, though at the most popular shows it may be necessary to split into twos and threes.

Each winter theaters open their doors for kids to see a Broadway show for free. Just bring a full-paying adult to specially designated performances. For more information on this cool annual event, called Kids Night on Broadway, visit the Web site, www.kidsnightonbroadway.com.

If you like Broadway you may also like Kupferberg Center Performances (#40).

MAKE THE MOST OF YOUR TIME Most
theaters are dark one day of the week, usually Monday, so plan your theater excursion accordingly. Scoring tickets for Tuesday through Thursday evening performances and Wednesday matinees is often easiest. Also check for those shows now offering an early (7 PM) curtain time on Tuesday. Do not buy tickets sold on the street; they may be illegally obtained and may not be honored at theater box offices.

BRONX ZOO

The Bronx Zoo is the country's largest metropolitan wildlife park, home to more than 4,500 animals, including endangered and threatened species. But the exhibits here aren't fenced areas containing standard zoo animals. One example is the World of Darkness, where your children are suddenly up way past their bedtimes to get a "night view" of such nocturnal animals as leopard cats, cloud rats, and bats. Kids can peek at a subterranean naked mole rat colony or watch big and beautiful endangered cats through the glass at Tiger Mountain, a not-to-be-missed exhibit. Keepers do daily demonstrations with the Siberian tigers as well as Tiger Talks three times daily. Other daily demonstrations to delight your children of all ages include the Sea Lion Feedings at 11 and 3 (except Wednesday) and indoor Primate Training at 2:30 from November through March and at 3:30 April through October.

The 265-acre zoo is too big to cover in a day and big enough to warrant returning again and again. With young children, begin in the north in parking lot B (the only year-round lot). Walk west to the Monkey House and loop around the sea lions to the Children's Zoo,

MAKE THE MOST OF YOUR TIME Summer sees the biggest crowds, and many exhibits—the monorail, SkyFari, camel rides, and Zoo Shuttle—are open only in warm months. (If you have small children, sit in the monorail's back row, so they can see.) In hot (or cold) weather, visit the indoor, temperature-controlled exhibits. Indoor exhibits perfect for rainy days include Aquatic Birds, the World of Birds, the World of Darkness, Reptiles, the Mouse House, and the Monkey House. From April through October, for an additional fee, visit the Butterfly Garden with more than 1,000 winged wonders.

Bronx River Pkwy. and
Fordham Rd., Bronx

 718/367–1010; www.wcs.org,
www.bronxzoo.com

 $14 ages 13 and up, $10 children
3–12, children 2 and under free;
rates change seasonally and annually; some attractions and
special exhibits extra

 Apr–Oct, M–F 10–5, Sa–Su and
holidays 10–5:30; Nov–Mar, daily
10–4:30; Children's Zoo Apr–Oct

 1 and up, Children's Zoo
8 and under

where kids can climb a giant spider's web, try on a turtle shell, or escape like a lizard down a hollow tree. The entire family will enjoy a bird's-eye view of the park, riding the SkyFari aerial cable car or the awesome Wild Asia Monorail (May–October weather-permitting). Head to these first because lines can get long. Look for the World of Reptiles as you pass. It's the only building from the zoo's opening day (November 8, 1899) serving its original purpose.

Wild Asia will appeal to children 8 and up who will want to experience JungleWorld, a major indoor exhibit that re-creates forests with about 780 animals representing 99 species. The Congo Gorilla Forest, a 6.5-acre indoor–outdoor African rain forest, takes visitors into the world of endangered lowland gorillas, African rock pythons, and other spectacular species. It's a must-see.

If you like this sight you may also like the Queens Zoo (#13).

EATS FOR KIDS Snack stands are throughout the park, selling (often overpriced) drinks, ice cream, and every other zoo snack imaginable. For more sub-stantial fare, eat at the **Asia Plaza, Terrace Café,** or **African Market** (over-looking the Baboon Reserve); these locations are open seasonally. The **Dancing Crane Café,** open year-round, features a contemporary menu that includes fresh pizza, salads, sandwiches, wraps, and Italian entrées. The café can seat 210 in-doors and 824 outdoors, overlooking the flamingo pond. Tables are available for those who pack a picnic.

KEEP IN MIND
A large rain puddle, a surly large sow, and my daughter once met with dire consequences on a fateful day. No change of clothes meant a muddy, uncomfortable morning for both mother and child. Dress for success and always carry a spare set of clothes in a ziplock in your bag, stroller, or car.

BROOKLYN ACADEMY OF MUSIC

Founded in 1861, the Brooklyn Academy of Music (BAM) is America's oldest performing arts center, presenting a full schedule of traditional and contemporary performing arts in the fields of dance, music, theater, opera, and cinema.

Public programs include BAMfamily weekend performances and spoken-word performances by and for teens. This great introduction to dance, music, and theater in beautiful theaters at affordable prices appeals to tots, teens, and parents alike. Performances are chosen to meet several criteria, including cultural diversity, multidisciplinary appeal, exposure to theatrical innovation, and the extent to which the performance is likely to introduce a young audience to art forms they may not have had the opportunity to experience before.

EATS FOR KIDS Try the **BAMcafé** (tel. 718/636–4139). Call ahead for restaurant hours, which change according to event and season. Visit **67 Burger** (67 Lafayette Ave., tel. 718/797–7150) for tasty sliders, salads, and fries. **Scopello** (63 Lafayette Ave., tel. 718 852–1100) has modern Italian dishes.

Fun for toddlers to early teens, the Brooklyn Academy of Music's annual BAMkids Film Festival, in the main building's BAM Rose Cinemas, includes a range of film fun from animated shorts of four to seven minutes to feature films running 1½ to 2 hours. A different

MAKE THE MOST OF YOUR TIME To reach BAM by car, take the Manhattan Bridge to Flatbush Avenue, and turn left onto Fulton Street. For the Harvey Theater, parking is on your right; for the Opera House, proceed two blocks on Fulton, and turn right onto Ashland Place. Parking is one block ahead on the right. (Hint: it's cheaper for subscribers and Friends of BAM.) If you're coming by subway, take the 2, 3, 4, 5, B, or Q line to Atlantic Avenue; the D, N, R, or M line to Pacific Street; the G line to Fulton Street; or C line to Lafayette Avenue. When there are no live events at the Opera House or Harvey Theater, you can park for 3 hours for $5.

30 Lafayette Ave., Brooklyn

  Concerts $10

 Year-round; call for schedule

718/636-4100; www.bam.org

5 and up, film festival 2–13

menu of weekday after-school programs appealing to middle schoolers and high schoolers throughout the year also offers the opportunity to learn about the visual arts, courtroom drama, and film critique.

Summertime means free R&B concerts at Brooklyn's downtown MetroTech Center and in area parks. And in addition to food, the BAMcafé serves up live jazz on Friday and Saturday nights. The BAM Harvey Theater is a renovated historic space two blocks from the main facility, at 651 Fulton Street, also used for performances and special events.

If you like this sight you may also like Kupferberg Center Performances (#40).

KEEP IN MIND Part of the fun of the spring BAMkids Film Festival is watching movies from other lands. A recent festival included 46 live-action and animated films from 22 countries including France, Brazil, Peru, the Netherlands, India, Taiwan, and Cameroon. But don't worry if you can't speak the language. Many foreign films have English subtitles, and for most of these films, actors read the subtitles out loud. The festival also includes live performances, discussions with filmmakers, and the BAMmies, where kids vote for their favorite films.

BROOKLYN BOTANIC GARDEN

Like bees to pollen or butterflies to blossoms, children take to the Brooklyn Botanic Garden like peas to a pod. This 52-acre blooming paradise with more than 10,000 plants outside and under glass heralds something new in nature to see each season: the Zen-like tranquillity of the Japanese Hill and Pond Garden in fall, the puffy winter pussy willows and early bulbs bursting with color in the Rock Garden in February, a spring flowering festival of tulips, or sunny summer garden delights. The Children's Garden—the oldest such garden within a botanic garden—has been welcoming families here since 1913.

The Discovery Garden is an outdoor adventure for kids, especially preschoolers, but filled with fun for everyone. It's immediately inside the Flatbush Avenue entrance at the south end of the garden. Children can explore sense-ational plants and colorful flowers, follow butterflies and birds in a wildlife meadow, pump water down a bamboo waterfall to a stream, hide under a tree, hike a nature trail, and meet a giant green spider. Teens in grades 8–12 from the Garden Apprentice Program staff the brightly colored Plant Discovery carts,

MAKE THE MOST OF YOUR TIME Not only are children under 12 free here, but senior citizens are free on Friday, year-round, so bring the grandparents. Saturday is also free 10–12 except on days when special public programs are scheduled. Mid-November through February it's also a free-for-all, so consider checking out the garden as it prepares for winter. An art and garden combination ticket can be purchased ($14 adults, $7 children 12 and over) to gain admission to the Brooklyn Botanic Garden as well as the Brooklyn Museum. Call the Brooklyn Central Library (Grand Army Plaza, tel. 718/230–2100) to see what's on their calendar and make a day of it.

providing fun opportunities for children and parents to learn about plants through close observation, scientific observation, and hands-on fun. The Celebrity Path is paved with stones inscribed with the names of famous Brooklynites past and present. How many can you recognize? The Japanese Hill and Pond Garden is home to ducks, turtles, koi, and herons, which can be surveyed from the Viewing Pavilion. Shrines, bridges, and waterfalls complete a miniaturized landscape that appeals to children. A restoration of this area has resulted in better paths for strollers and wheelchairs.

Free drop-in programs such as Discovery Tuesdays, Thirsty Garden Thursdays, Storytelling Saturdays, and Tree-mendous Trees are held daily for children and their adult companions to experience hands-on gardening and crafts to take and make.

If you like this site you may also like the New York Botanical Garden (#27).

KEEP IN MIND Did you know that fragrance is the strongest of the senses to trigger memory? To help your children explore the family connection that a garden provides visit the Herb Garden. Here you can find plants you know, but also curious or different herbs from around the world. These plants may stir up memories for you, your parents, and your children. Perhaps a grandmother might share a bit of her early childhood in Italy or a plant may remind a grandfather of his native Poland, fueling conversation and learning for a grandchild.

EATS FOR KIDS
Picnicking isn't allowed in the garden. Try the on-site **Terrace Café,** which serves lunch outdoors from spring to early fall and in the Steinhardt Conservatory late fall and winter. For deli sandwiches and cheesecake, take a short ride to **Junior's Restaurant** (386 Flatbush Ave., tel. 718/852–5257), a classic '50s diner.

BROOKLYN CHILDREN'S MUSEUM

F ounded in 1899 (and, as of this writing, slated to reopen its renovated space in Spring 2008), this was the world's first museum for children and has since served as a model for other children's museums worldwide, thanks to interactive exhibits, kids' programs, workshops, and performances. The new L-shape building is also slated to be the first "green" children's museum in the city. From geothermal wells to solar panels, many aspects of the environmentally friendly design will be incorporated into the Museum's educational programs.

Upon arrival, check the daily information board to see a listing of workshops and programs. From the neon "People Tube" at the entrance, visitors will have a sweeping view of Neighborhood Nature, a 7,000 square foot natural science exhibit with Brooklyn habitats including a freshwater pond and a woodland field. Be sure to visit Fantasia, the Museum's 20-foot-long bright yellow albino Burmese python along with an array of other snakes, turtles, and other live reptiles. Then head to any of the 10 galleries, which incorporate

KEEP IN MIND The Planet Brooklyn culture series spotlights a different culture every month with a museum-wide celebration of a special holiday, festival, or tradition. Free Friday Rooftop Jam offers dance and theater performances every Friday evening in July and August.

EATS FOR KIDS Visit the new **Kids Café** in the museum, which also opens onto the rooftop terrace for outdoor dining in good weather. Or try **Kingston Pizza** (259 Kingston Ave., tel. 718/774–7665) for a cheesy slice of pizza. **Eastern Chinese** (127 Kingston Ave., tel. 718/735–3408) with Szechuan, Hunan, and Cantonese family favorites, is also nearby.

145 Brooklyn Ave., Brooklyn

 718/735-4400;
www.brooklynkids.org

 Suggested donation $5

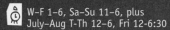 W–F 1–6, Sa–Su 11–6, plus
July–Aug T–Th 12–6, Fri 12–6:30

 18 mth and up

musical traditions, nature experiments, live animals, collections, and computers to create exhibits that tickle the imaginations of young and old. On any given day, your children may be able to assemble an 8-foot-high elephant skeleton puzzle, play musical instruments from around the world, pet a snake from the live animal collection, or experiment with plants.

Head to World Brooklyn, a 4,000 square foot exhibit highlighting the many vibrant cultures that call Brooklyn home. It includes a streetscape of interactive storefronts from Brooklyn's own ethnic neighborhoods. Create a colorful costume for Caribbean Carnival, dish up a pretend pie at the pizzeria, or bake bread in the Mexican bakery. There's much to do here for all ages but kids 5 and under will claim Totally Tots as a place all their own. It incorporates the museum's natural science and cultural collections in a wonderland of sand and water play, climbing structures, art spaces, a reading nook, and a theater.

If you like this sight you may also like the Children's Museum of Manhattan (#54).

MAKE THE MOST OF YOUR TIME Take a break
at Brower Park behind the museum, surrounded by St. Marks, Brooklyn, and Kingston avenues and Prospect Place. It's a great place to take a picnic, relax on the benches, or play in the playground. Also close by is the new Jewish Children's Museum (792 Eastern Parkway, tel. 718/467-0600, M–Th 10–4, Su 10–6). With its Gallery of Games, a game show studio, miniature golf with a course highlighting Jewish life-cycle events, and hands-on exhibits celebrating Jewish holidays, biblical history, and the land of Israel, it's a museum like no other.

BROOKLYN MUSEUM

It's the second-largest museum in New York State, established in 1823, and considered one of the premier art institutions in the world. Is it in Manhattan? No, it was born and bred—and still lives—in Brooklyn. It's the beaux arts–style Brooklyn Museum. More than one million objects range from the art of ancient Egypt to contemporary painting and sculpture, and the museum's collections of Asian, American, Egyptian, Native American, and African art are recognized as some of the best in the world.

Check out the Dinner Party, a multimedia installation by Judy Chicago in the Elizabeth Sackler Center for Feminist Art. This fascinating work includes 39 ornate place settings at a table representing prominent women in history. Weekend family programs are free with museum admission. Each session offers different 90-minute programs during which families explore the galleries, enjoy an activity, and make their own art.

MAKE THE MOST OF YOUR TIME The museum is near the Brooklyn Botanic Garden (see #62), the main branch of the Brooklyn Public Library, and Prospect Park and its zoo (see #s 17 and 16). Although you could easily spend a day at the museum, it's probably better, especially with young children, to keep your first visit short. Spend half a day here, wander to 7th Avenue for lunch at one of the restaurants or cafés, and visit another nearby destination in the afternoon. It'll break up the day and leave your children with a positive memory of the museum.

200 Eastern Pkwy., Brooklyn

 Suggested donation $8 adults, $4 students and seniors, children under 12 free

 W–F 10–5, Sa–Su 11–6, 1st Sa of mth 11–11

718/638–5000; www.brooklynart.org, www.brooklynmuseum.org/education

 4 and up, Arty Facts 4–7, Gallery/ Studio Program 6 and up

The Gallery/Studio Program, for ages 6 up to and including adults, offers the opportunity to study the museum's diverse collections as well as work in the studio on their own art. Courses in drawing, painting, sculpture, abstract art, printmaking, collage, digital photography, and mixed media are offered in 8- and 10-week sessions. Students then get to exhibit their art in the Museum's Education Gallery! Scholarships and work–study opportunities are also available.

If you like this sight you may also like the Museum of Modern Art (#34).

KEEP IN MIND
The Museum's premier event for all ages, First Saturdays, takes place 5–11 PM every month except September. Don't make a day of it. Make a night of it! This family-friendly event is free, and features music in the galleries, art-making projects, films, performances, gallery talks, and ends with a dance party. Flat-rate parking is a bargain after 5 PM.

EATS FOR KIDS The **Museum Café** is open almost as long as the museum, or try the **Second Street Café** (*see* the Prospect Park Zoo, #16). For a snack and a drink, try **Ozzie's Coffee & Tea** (57 7th Ave., tel. 718/398–6695), an interesting converted drugstore with apothecary cases. **Tom's Restaurant** (782 Washington Ave., tel. 718 636–9738) is a quick walk and has kid-friendly family fare.

CARNEGIE HALL

How do you get to Carnegie Hall? Practice . . . practice . . . or just attend one of the family concerts held throughout the year on weekend afternoons on this world-famous stage and in Zankel Hall, underneath the main hall.

The popular family concert series, which began here in 1995, introduces children to classical, jazz, and folk music at affordable, family-friendly prices. Preconcert activities on the main stage and in other smaller Carnegie Hall spaces include storytelling, hands-on musical experiences, and instrument demonstrations. Concertgoers ages 5 to 12 will especially enjoy the KidsNotes program, with activities and information about each family concert.

Another worthy concert program, the McGraw-Hill Companies CarnegieKIDS, is designed to introduce music to preschool children. It's aimed at nursery schools, day care centers, kindergarten classes, Headstart programs, and small groups, but is also open to families; advance registration is required. These interactive performances last about 45 minutes

MAKE THE MOST OF YOUR TIME

At select Carnegie Hall performances, usually excluding the family concert series, you can purchase partial view seats for $10 each from noon until one hour before the show with a limit of two tickets per patron on a first-come, first-served basis.

EATS FOR KIDS Before a concert or at intermission, visit the **Citi Café**, on the Parquet level, for light fare or desserts. The Zankel Hall Bar outside the auditorium also has light fare and drinks. Or whistle a happy tune over to **Brooklyn Diner** (212 W. 57th St., tel. 212/581–8900). Go for the generous portions of kid and comfort foods or the decadent desserts. You can also order the quintessential corned beef on rye and bowl of matzoh ball soup at the **Carnegie Deli** (854 7th Ave., tel. 212/757–2245).

154 W. 57th St., at 7th Ave.

212/247-7800, 212/903-9765 tour schedule updates; www.carnegiehall.org

Family concerts $8; tour $10 adults, $7 students, $3 children 11 and under

Tour M–F 11:30, 2, and 3, Sa 11:30 and 12:30, Su 12:30 during concert season, performances permitting

 Family concerts 5 and up, the McGraw-Hill Companies CarnegieKIDS 3–6, tour 7 and up

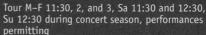

and are ideal for children ages 3–6. These concerts are not held in the main hall, however, but rather in the Kaplan space on the fifth floor.

To make a concert experience special for your children, discuss any famous musicians that you or other family members have seen perform here. Headliners have been playing Carnegie Hall since 1891, when its opening concert series included none other than Tchaikovsky conducting his own works. Remind your teens that you weren't actually at *that* performance.

One-hour guided tours of the hall are also given. And if your kids want to get a close-up look at Benny Goodman's clarinet or catch a glimpse of Arturo Toscanini's baton, visit the Rose Museum, open daily 11–4:30 during the concert season as well as to concert patrons in the evening.

If you like this site you may also like the Brooklyn Academy of Music (#63).

KEEP IN MIND Can't get to Carnegie Hall? Let Carnegie Hall come to you! Since 1976, the Neighborhood Concert Series, a program of the Weill Music Institute at Carnegie Hall, has hosted free one-hour community concerts in public libraries, community and senior centers, and shelters in all five New York City boroughs. A variety of artists and ensembles performing repertoires from classical and jazz to folk and pop make up each Neighborhood Concert season. Best of all, some of these concerts are Workshop Concerts or Kids Concerts. Seating is on a first-come, first-served basis.

CASTLE CLINTON NATIONAL MONUMENT

Like any good castle, Castle Clinton has a long history. It was built before the beginning of the War of 1812 to defend the city from sea assault, but no attack ever came. Today you can admire the views of the Statue of Liberty and Ellis Island while your children look for gun ports and scan the stone walls, imagining themselves soldiers defending a city.

Originally named the Southwest Battery, this circular redbrick fortress served as U.S. Army headquarters during the War of 1812. It had a timber causeway with a drawbridge connecting the fort to Manhattan and was equipped with 28 guns and a magazine inside the rounded ends of the rear wall. In 1817 it was renamed to honor the city's mayor, DeWitt Clinton. Today National Park Service rangers dressed in period costume are available to answer questions, and exhibits tell of the setting's many lives.

It's hard to imagine a more varied history. In 1824 the site was turned into an elegant entertainment facility known as Castle Garden, where the "Swedish Nightingale," Jenny Lind, sang in 1850. From 1855 to 1890, it served as a receiving station for more than 8

MAKE THE MOST OF YOUR TIME You cannot directly drive here. Nearby parking is nearly impossible and expensive. Consider public transportation. You can take a subway to South Ferry or Bowling Green or take the bus or Staten Island Ferry to Battery Park. Castle Clinton is also a visitor center for the city's national parks. Pick up a brochure and visit another national historic site or take a walk to the South Street Seaport. Fascinated with high-rise buildings? Visit the nearby Skyscraper Museum at 39 Battery Place. It's open Wednesday through Sunday from 12 to 6. Admission is $5 for adults and $2.50 for students (tel. 212/968–1961).

million immigrants and from 1896 to 1941 housed the New York Aquarium. Today it functions as a restored fort, museum, and ticket office for ferries to the Statue of Liberty and Ellis Island. If you have young children in tow, you may find it easier to take a self-guided tour (20–30 minutes). Children 7 and older may be up for a ranger-led tour (20–60 minutes). A kiosk on the parade grounds has an information desk and a bookstore filled with books on the history of New York.

Look for the bronze statue titled *The Immigrants,* depicting a Jewish man bent in prayer with his family, along with a priest, a freed African-American slave, a worker, and a child. In all, more than 300 years of history can be discovered on the grounds.

If you like this sight you may also like the Federal Hall National Memorial (#46).

KEEP IN MIND
Castle Clinton is only one of six historic National Park Service units in New York City. The others include Federal Hall National Memorial and the Theodore Roosevelt Birthplace (*see* #46 and #3), St. Paul's National Historic Site, General Grant National Memorial, and the Hamilton Grange National Memorial.

EATS FOR KIDS For dependable, kid-friendly fare—burgers, wraps, and fajitas—try **T.G.I. Friday's** (47 Broadway, tel. 212/483–8322, with other locations all around the city). **Zaytuna** (17 Battery Pl., tel. 212/871–8300) is an eclectic buffet of everything from sushi to pizza, pita to ice cream.

CENTRAL PARK

57

Central Park is to New York as the sun is to the solar system. This green oasis of more than 840 acres is a magnet for families, joggers, bikers, strollers (on foot and wheels), skaters, sunbathers, and people-watchers. Where else in the city can you go horseback riding, boating, ice-skating, roller-skating, folk dancing, fishing, and bird-watching; visit the zoo; and attend a play, puppet show, concert, and ball game—though probably not in one day? Weekends are busy here (but crowds make it safe), and free entertainment is everywhere. Start at the Dairy Visitor Center and Gift Shop (65th St., mid-park, tel. 212/794–6564) where exhibits and interactive videos provide an introduction to the park. For the toddler set, there are a plethora of playgrounds to choose from. Head to 67th Street and 5th Avenue for the tree house playground. A playground at 99th Street (east side) accommodates children with disabilities. The Ancient Playground at E. 85th mirrors the theme of the Egyptian Wing of the nearby Metropolitan Museum.

MAKE THE MOST OF YOUR TIME

The Loeb Boathouse (E. 72nd and Park Dr. N, tel. 212/517–2233) also rents bikes (with helmets) and rowboats and kayaks (with life jackets), daily 10–6 on a first-come, first-served basis. Call ahead to inquire about gondola rides M–F 5–9 and Sa and Su 2–9).

On land: A must is a ride on the 1903 Friedsam Memorial Carousel (Center Dr. and 65th St., tel. 212/879–0244). Belvedere Castle (79th St. Transverse, tel. 212/772–0210),

EATS FOR KIDS Try the **Loeb Boathouse Cafe**, a seasonal open-air restaurant on the water; a nearby cafeteria serving breakfast and lunch; or the **Sheep Meadow Café** (Central Park at W. 69th St., tel. 212/396–4100), also called Mineral Springs. For a splurge, visit famous **Tavern on the Green** (Central Park West at 67th St., tel. 212/873–3200). Twinkling lights, glitzy glass, and mirrors captivate young audiences. Pretheater specials are reasonable, but reservations are a must.

Bordered by 5th Ave., Central Park West, 59th St., and 110th St.

 212/360-3444; www.centralparknyc.org

Free; some attractions charge

Daily sunrise–sunset

All ages

home of a weather station and the Henry Luce Nature Observatory, houses nature exhibits and programs. Swedish Cottage (79th St. Transverse, tel. 212/988-9093), an 1876 schoolhouse, holds marionette performances, also a popular stop for youngsters 2–10. Year-round performances are usually less than an hour and tickets are $6.

On or near water: At Conservatory Water (off 5th Ave. at 74th St.), children pose by literary statues. Summer storytelling takes place Saturday at 11, model boat races Saturday at 10 spring–fall. To skate on frozen water, try the Wollman Memorial Rink (6th Ave. at 59th St., tel. 212/396-1010), mid-October–March (in-line skating April–September), or Lasker Rink (off Lenox Ave. and 110th St., tel. 212/534-7639)—a pool in summer. Tired yet?

If you like this sight you may also like Prospect Park (#17).

KEEP IN MIND It's not just couples who like horse-drawn carriage rides. Kids love them, too. You can see the carriages assembled on Central Park South (59th St. between 5th Ave. and Ave. of the Americas) and outside Tavern on the Green. Each is decorated distinctively, and the drivers, too, are a colorful group. Some even sport top hats. Day and evening rides are available for about $40 for 20 minutes for up to four passengers. For more information, contact Central Park Carriage Rides (tel. 212/246-0520).

CENTRAL PARK ZOO

Approximately 1,500 animals represent more than 120 species in this indefatigably charming 6½-acre zoo, a perfect destination for little ones. It's walkable and stroller-friendly, and even the youngest tot can see the animals from low-lying or low-sitting carriages. Three climatic regions—the Rain Forest, Temperate Territory, and Polar Circle—form the focal points.

The Rain Forest is a veritable jungle, filled with the sounds and swirling mist of a roaring waterfall and the calls of tropical birds. Older children like the piranha aquarium and the colobus monkeys. A way-cool sight in the Temperate Territory is an island of Japanese snow monkeys in a lake with black-neck swans. Speaking of cool, the Polar Circle contains some exhibits refrigerated to 34°F. Look for arctic foxes as well as the ever-popular penguins, puffins, and polar bears, whose natural habitats feature 10 viewing areas with above- and below-water views. Don't miss penguin feeding time daily at 10:30 and 2:30. Tuxedos optional. It's a highlight of any zoo visit along with the Sea Lion feedings at 1:30, 2, and 4 PM.

MAKE THE MOST OF YOUR TIME Special community events like
National Pig Day, Boo at the Zoo, and Chill Out with the Polar Bears and Penguins are sched-uled throughout the year, free with general admission. An interactive preschool series for children 3–5 with an adult is offered for a fee in various sessions throughout the year. Children's and family programs (some with charges) for youngsters 6 and up have included such favorites as Breakfast with the Birds, Snooze at the Zoo, Rainforest Retreat, and Spooky Species.

Central Park at 64th St. and 5th Ave.

 212/439-6500;
www.centralparkzoo.org

 $8 ages 13 and up,
$3 children 3–12, free
under 3; some programs
extra

 Early Apr–late Oct, M–F 10–5,
Sa–Su 10:30–5:30; late Oct–early
Apr, daily 10–4:30

All ages

For the 6-and-under crowd, no visit here is complete without a side trip to the Tisch Children's Zoo. Children can explore touch boxes, hear through huge rabbit ears, examine giant turtle shells and eggs, observe waterfowl from behind a child-size duck blind, and pet and feed many animals. Small animal sculptures moo, baa, or grunt when touched by little hands.

From May through September don't miss costumed animal characters who mingle with visitors. The Acorn Theater presents shows using puppets, costumed characters, music, and song to teach basic animal facts. Where else could you hear the "Metamorphosis Boogie" or participate in a Wildlife Workout?

If you like this sight you may also like the Prospect Park Zoo (#16)

KEEP IN MIND
Videotaping the antics of animals or the antics of loved ones interacting with the animals is enjoyable even when the idea of family togetherness is uncool. Disposable cameras for young ones, too, is a fun and practical way to sustain interest.

EATS FOR KIDS Children go wild for snacks at the zoo's indoor-outdoor **Leaping Frog Cafe.** It has kids' value meals with keepsake bags and "did you know" table tents with facts about food at the zoo. Central Park also has food stands near many entrances. You may recognize the pricey **Loeb Boathouse Cafe** (East Park Dr. and E. 72nd St., tel. 212/517–2233) from such movies as *Three Men and a Little Lady* and *When Harry Met Sally;* open March–September.

CHELSEA PIERS

Chelsea Piers has been called Manhattan's ultimate playground with spectacular views. After opening in 1995, it became the fourth-most-visited destination in the city (4.1 million visitors in 2000) in five years, behind the Statue of Liberty and Ellis Island, the Metropolitan Museum of Art, and Madison Square Garden. As incongruous as it sounds, your family can ice-skate in summer and play golf all winter, all on piers jutting into the Hudson River. The piers date back to 1910, part of nine piers that were a popular port of call for grand ocean liners. In 1994 the Chelsea Piers were restored and revitalized, and construction of the complex began.

The first thing to do is pick an activity. The Toddler Adventure Center, an interactive play center for toddlers 3 and under will occupy your preschoolers for hours right up until naptime! Batting cages, golf, bowling, or ice skating are sure bets for all ages in your family. Teens will particularly enjoy the climbing wall, bowling, or basketball with or without adults. The Field House (between Piers 61 and 62, tel. 212/336–6500) is an 80,000-square-

MAKE THE MOST OF YOUR TIME

At the 1-mile Waterside Promenade you can stroll, grab a bench, or just relax and enjoy the spectacular Hudson River views. Once it reopens in fall 2008, the Intrepid, Sea, Air and Space Museum (Pier 86, W. 46th St., 212/245–0072) will be worth incorporating into your day.

EATS FOR KIDS **Chelsea Brewing Company** (Pier 59, tel. 212/336–6440), overlooking the marina, features casual riverside pub fare, including gourmet pizzas and pasta, indoors or out. For breakfast, lunch, or an evening meal, try the pastries and sandwiches at **Ruthy's Bakery & Café** (Main Plaza, Pier 62, tel. 212/336–6666), or take home a special-occasion cake for (you know) a special occasion. **300 New York** has grill menu items made to order. You can also picnic along the promenade at **Jason's Riverside Grill** (Pier 60, tel. 212/989–8400).

23rd St. and Hudson River

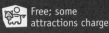 Free; some attractions charge

 Daily 24 hrs; attraction hrs vary

 212/336–6666; www.chelseapiers.com

6 mth and up, but varies by attraction

foot facility for gymnastics, team sports, basketball, and soccer. It contains four batting cages; dance studios; a martial arts mezzanine; and a 30-foot climbing wall designed for children, teens, and adult beginners. 300 New York (between Piers 59 and 60, tel. 212/835–BOWL) is a 40-lane facility equipped with automatic scoring on plasma screens and the Golf Club at Chelsea Piers (Pier 59, tel. 212/336–6400) houses 52 heated and weather-protected hitting stalls on four levels.

Chelsea Piers has great walk-in activities for get-up-and-go fun anytime. Toddlers to teens can try general skating sessions at Sky Rink (Pier 61, tel. 212/336–6100). Young and old duffers can tee off at the Golf Club's driving range. Softball, T-ball, and baseball fans can work on their swing at the Field House batting cage.

If you like this sight you may also like Asphalt Green (#66).

KEEP IN MIND If you decide to take a stroll while your old-enough offspring pursue other activities, plan to meet up later at a specific time at an agreed-upon, no-fail place. As this recreational mecca is vast, you could be pacing the piers for hours if you don't have a plan.

CHILDREN'S MUSEUM OF MANHATTAN

One of the magical things about this museum is that there's always something new to see. Exhibits in the five floors of exhibition space change frequently; the likes of Clifford, Dora the Explorer, and Dr. Seuss have anchored some popular exhibits here.

Weather permitting from May through October, don't miss City Splash in the Sussman Environmental Center. This outdoor water-play area invites young visitors to explore the physical properties of water as they splash, pour, float, and play. It's a must-see. You may want to bring a change of clothes or towel, however, in case of excessive splashing. And take extra care on the stairs leading to this play area.

Children 18 months to 4 years will love the interactive PlayWorks™ exhibition, where they can feed alphabet letters to a talking baby dragon, drive an NYC fire truck, paint on a 6-foot art wall, make their way through a crawling challenge course, or connect an air tub puzzle.

MAKE THE MOST OF YOUR TIME For children 5 or older, be
sure to sign up for a workshop in the Creativity Lab, where you can explore the visual and performing arts, science, and literacy. Noted artists, writers, chefs, and educators from all walks of life present workshops here on the weekends, holidays, and in summer. Local authors and illustrators often read from their newly published works and performances include Broadway artists, professional dance troupes, and recording artists.

Tisch Building, 212 W. 83rd St.

 $9 ages 1 and up

T–Su 10–5, T and Th 10–8

212/721–1234; www.cmom.org

Infants–10

Two circle times each day are offered here for children 4 and younger with songs, stories, movement, and surprise sensory box exploration. Keep an eye on the schedule for special author readings in PlayWorks™ Reads. Sing-alongs, art projects to make and take, and fun-for-the-whole-family performances by artists like Blue Man Group are just a few of the programs offered throughout the year. Call ahead or check the Web site to see what's scheduled for the day you visit, or check the posted schedule of events as soon as you arrive. Then head first to the areas that pique your child's interest the most.

KEEP IN MIND
So much to do, so little time? Leave the stroller at home or in the car and avoid the long lines at the coat–stroller check.

If you like this site, you may also like the Children's Museum of the Arts (#53).

EATS FOR KIDS **EJ's Luncheonette** (447 Amsterdam Ave., tel. 212/ 873–3444) offers a 10% discount to Children's Museum of Manhattan members. Go for the blue-plate special or the skinless chicken. For a heaping helping of deli delights, visit **Artie's New York Delicatessen** (2290 Broadway, at 83rd St., tel. 212/579–5959).

CHILDREN'S MUSEUM OF THE ARTS

I t's hard to know where to begin when entering this small SoHo museum, but somehow children manage. They set their own pace, find a space that interests them, and move on, often returning to their favorite workshop or exhibit. The focus here is hands-on art, based on the theory that children learn best by doing. And they do . . . and do. In 5,000 square feet of kid-comfortable space, they touch, create, and explore.

There's always something new here, as exhibitions rotate every three months, highlighting such themes as art from around the world or local book illustrators. The permanent collection includes more than 2,000 paintings and drawings from more than 50 countries. Daily workshops follow the themes of color, line, and form and always include a painting project, sculpture activity, and work using found objects, reinforcing that art can and should be made out of everything.

Your children can draw on computers, developing computer skills, artistic sensibilities, and hand-eye coordination without even realizing it. For older kids, the Artist's Studio

MAKE THE MOST OF YOUR TIME

The innovative WEE-Arts Early Childhood program (Wondrous, Experimenting, and Exploring artists), held Wednesday–Friday 10:45–12 year-round, is a drop-in program for 1- to 3-year-olds ($20 for a group/family of three)—a favorite with the toddler set.

EATS FOR KIDS In the mood for waffles any time of day? Visit the **Cupping Room Cafe** (359 W. Broadway, tel. 212/925–2898). Three-course, prix-fixe dinners (Monday and Tuesday) and weekend brunch are also treats. For a hip, moderately priced artist hangout, try **Jerry's** (101 Prince St., tel. 212/966–9464). Another eatery close and big enough to accommodate families is **Spring Street Natural Restaurant** (62 Spring St., 212/966–0290) for healthy, organic food at affordable prices.

 182 Lafayette St.

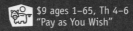 $9 ages 1–65, Th 4–6
"Pay as You Wish"

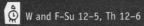 W and F–Su 12–5, Th 12–6

 1–10

212/274-0986; www.cmany.org

features daily art projects involving problem solving and exploration with a variety of art materials. It's not unusual to find artists from the community working side by side with the next artistic generation here. Meanwhile, younger visitors can enjoy the Creative Play Area, which includes a ball pond, theater, and green screen.

Workshops in music, dance, theater, and puppetry instill confidence and foster skill mastery, open-ended exploration, and creativity. Check out the summer weeklong art camps and fall after-school programs for kids 6–12. Call ahead for info on daily music programs. Paintings, sculptures, and drawings from museum visitors, adult artists, and children from around the world are displayed throughout the museum.

If you like this site you may also like the Children's Museum of Manhattan (#54).

KEEP IN MIND Need to shake the sillies out? Children as young as 2 and as old as 8 will want to jump into the Ball Pond, a carpeted area filled with large, brightly colored physioballs. Test the waters before your kids dive right into the Ball Pond! If older children are the big fish in the pond, wait until they clear out before allowing your little guppies to "swim." It's also not advisable to send toddlers into the ball pit in sandals or loose-fitting shoes unless you're prepared to wade in yourself and spend 15–20 minutes searching for lost footwear.

CLAY PIT PONDS STATE PARK PRESERVE

New York City's only state park preserve, these 260 natural acres near Staten Island's southwest shore were once the site of a clay-mining operation (hence the name). But to really tell its history, you have to go back to the Cretaceous period, nearly 70 million years ago, when sands and clays were deposited here. More recent glacial deposits, 12,000 years ago, add to the area's geological significance. But though the visitor center does have historical photos and a few artifacts, the main draw here is nature.

Young visitors will enjoy being on the lookout for snakes, box turtles, screech owls, fence lizards, raccoons, black-capped chickadees, toads, frogs, and spring peepers. More than 170 bird species can also be spotted here. Older children may enjoy taking along a trail guide pamphlet to help identify the flowers and landscape changes.

Established in 1977, the preserve harbors such diverse habitats as fields, sandy barrens, spring-fed streams, bogs, and other freshwater wetlands and woodlands, creating an oasis

KEEP IN MIND Trails are for feet or hooves only, not tires or paws. Watch for nonpoisonous snakes—garter, black racer, and water snakes—not because they'd hurt us (they won't). They're only a threat to the insect and rodent populations they keep in check. Do dress your children in sun hats, long sleeves, socks, and shoes to ward off bugs, ticks, and sun. Keep sunscreen and hats in the back of your car from spring to summer and always apply sunscreen liberally if you're spending an extended time outdoors.

83 Nielsen Ave., Staten Island

 Free; some programs charge

 718/967–1976;
www.nysparks.state.ny.us

 Daily sunrise–sunset,
parking lot M–Su 9–5

2 and up

amid an urban area and enabling city dwellers to commune with nature. Each season paints a different natural backdrop. Throughout the year, wildflowers or their dried silhouettes can be seen along the trails. White wild carrot flowers and Queen Anne's lace frame summer fields, folding up in winter to resemble tiny birds' nests. The wildflower garden behind headquarters is particularly colorful in spring, though some flowers blossom in late summer.

Hiking and horseback riding are permitted on designated trails. Take the Abraham's Pond Trail (blue markers) to the Ellis Swamp Trail (yellow markers) for a 1-mile walk, or stay on the Abraham's Pond Trail the entire way, a ½-mile jaunt. The Green Trail meanders through a mature hardwood forest.

If you like this sight you may also like Queens County Farm Museum (#14).

MAKE THE MOST OF YOUR TIME

Explore on a Saturday and also take in a program on gardening, animals, insects, or pond ecology. Some include arts and crafts projects to take home. Call ahead to learn the schedule. Visit nearby Historic Richmond Town or the Sandy Ground Historical Society Library and Museum (538 Woodrow Rd., tel. 718/317–5796) to make a day of it.

EATS FOR KIDS There are sheltered picnic tables behind preserve headquarters. German fare is on tap at Killmeyer's (4254 Arthur Kill Rd., tel. 718/984–1202). Weekend evenings and Sunday afternoons often bring an oompah band. The 1716 Old Bermuda Inn (2512 Arthur Kill Rd., tel. 718/948–7600) is a bit pricey for lunch and dinner, but the Sunday brunch is a good value.

CONEY ISLAND

Developed as a seaside resort in the early 19th century, Coney Island became famous as a growing amusement center in the 1880s. By the 1950s, it became less popular as a resort destination but steadily grew as a residential area. Today summer crowds still flock to the boardwalk, the 3-mile beach, the amusement park rides, and a seaside aquarium (New York Aquarium, #28). Fishing on the pier and a sports center offering ice-skating and indoor sports round out the fun. On warm and sunny days, you can find a lively mix here, with summer weekends the busiest times. Apartment dwellers come to escape the stifling summer heat, teenagers come for the thrill rides, and families flock to Coney Island with kids in tow to rekindle a memory and to create new ones for the next generation.

The historic Parachute Jump is no longer a ride, but it's the most visible and picturesque landmark on Coney Island. Its glory days may be gone, but Deno's Wonder Wheel Amusement Park (1025 Boardwalk, tel. 718/372–2592)—25 rides, two arcades, and an old-fashioned sweet shop—is still a family-friendly favorite. Many of the old attractions like Astroland

EATS FOR KIDS Consider a frank: After all, this is where **Nathan's Famous** made Coney Island hot dog history. For delectable pizza (pies only, no slices), particularly the white pie liberally strewn with garlic, try **Totonno's** (1524 Neptune between W. 15th and W. 16th, tel. 718/372–8606).

MAKE THE MOST OF YOUR TIME There are many individual (and sometimes questionable) ride operators up and down the boardwalk. These separate rides and attractions are not a centrally managed amusement park, so stick with Deno's. A real boon to the area and good news for sports fans is that baseball has returned to Brooklyn. The Brooklyn Cyclones, a minor league Class A affiliate of the New York Mets, takes to the field at the 6,500-seat KeySpan Park (1904 Surf Ave. between W. 16th and W. 19th Sts.). Tickets are pleasantly affordable ($5–$12) and can be ordered online at www.brooklyncyclones.com or by phone at 718/507–TIXX.

Southern tip of Brooklyn

Brooklyn Tourism and Visitors Center
(718/802–3846, www.visitbrooklyn.org);
Coney Island USA (718/372–5159,
www.coneyisland.com)

 Free; amusement park
rides vary; sideshows
$6 adults; $4 under 12;
museum 99¢

 Attraction hrs vary by season

1 and up

and the Carousel are gone, as the city's strategic blueprint for development unfolds. In the works are new attractions and redevelopment along the lines of Times Square with plans for a new amusement area as well.

Lively traditional circus sideshows, complete with a fire-eater, sword swallower, snake charmer, and contortionist, are featured at Sideshows by the Seashore, the last standing ten-in-one sideshow in the country (W. 12th St. and Surf Ave.). Upstairs from the sideshows, you can find the Coney Island Museum (open Friday–Sunday 12–5), which contains exhibits spotlighting historic Coney Island and related memorabilia. An extensive array of tourist information and literature is also available here.

If you like this sight you may also like Rye Playland (#10).

KEEP IN MIND A big draw for families and a hot spot for teens is the Seaside Summer Concerts on Thursday Nights at 7:30 at Asser Levy/Seaside Park at W. 5th Street and Surf Avenue. In you're not sneaking under the boardwalk, check out the Saturday Night Film Series at the Coney Island Museum (1208 Surf Ave.). It's free popcorn and only $5 to get in. Call 718/372–5101 for the schedule and to be sure the flick is a family pick.

EL MUSEO DEL BARRIO

El Museum del Barrio was founded in 1969 by artist and educator Rafael Montañez Ortiz out of concern that the Latino cultural experience was not represented in New York City's major museums. Today it's the city's only Latin museum dedicated to Puerto Rican, Caribbean, and Latin American art, and it's well worth experiencing.

The permanent collection, housed in a site that looks very much like an apartment building, contains 6,500 objects, including prints, drawings, paintings, sculpture, photographs, film, video, works on paper, and artifacts. Young visitors will enjoy the dolls, marks, miniatures, and musical instruments in the Traditional Arts collection. Older kids may particularly like the works on paper, as well as the Pre-Columbian collection of paintings and sculptures. A favorite piece of eye-catching color and energy is *La Cama,* a sculpture of an ornate bed by Pepon Osorion, created in 1987. You can't miss it and you wouldn't want to. Signage throughout the museum is in Spanish and English.

MAKE THE MOST OF YOUR TIME For a quiet stroll or calming break in your touring, visit Central Park's nearby Conservatory Garden (enter at 5th Ave. and 105th St.). Few know of the walkway under the pergola of this 6-acre formal garden that has medallions inscribed with the names of the original 13 states. Find the pergola by looking for the geyser fountain. It spouts in front.

1230 5th Ave.

212/831/7272;
www.elmuseo.org

 $6 ages 13 and up, $4
students, under 12 free

W–Su 11–5

5 and up

As important as the collection is, so too are the community events that highlight
the culture and strengthen this community. Summer Nites at El Museo is an annual
tradition with free live concerts throughout the summer that feature all types of
musical guests from women who rock to Latin funk to the Spanish Harlem Orchestra,
as well as an alternate music festival. Concerts are held in the beautifully restored
Teatro Heckscher, former home to Broadway tryouts in the 1930s and the original
site for the Joseph Papp New York Shakespeare Festival. Check out the restored
30-foot murals and stained-glass roundels.

Artist-led gallery activities and projects are free with advance registration. And
popular neighborhood walking tours geared toward adults and teens are held
on Saturday in April through October from 3 to 5 and are also free.

If you like this site you may also like the Schomburg Center (#9).

KEEP IN MIND A visit here should take about
two hours, leaving plenty of
time to catch a Children's Read
Aloud program at the Aguilar
Branch of the New York Public Library (174 E. 110th St., tel. 212/
534–2930) or other kids events frequently scheduled here. Also close
by is the Guggenheim Museum (1071
5th Ave., tel. 212/423–2500).

EATS FOR KIDS For breakfast, a light bite, or the delicious butter-
milk muffins filled with Tanzanian tropical fruit jam, head over to **Boma Coffe &
Tea Co.,** (2037 5th Ave., tel. 212/427–8668). For tapas and Puerto Rican palate
pleasers, try **Camaradasel Barrio Bar and Restaurant** (2241 1st Ave. at
115th Street, tel. 212/348–2703).

ELLIS ISLAND

A symbol of America's immigrant experience, Ellis Island welcomed some 12 million people into the United States from 1892 until 1954. Today their descendants make up almost 40% of the U.S. population, as well as many of the visitors here. Should you choose to join those millions and set foot on this landmark, you can discover or rediscover this important part of American history.

The Ellis Island Immigrant Museum tells the remarkable stories of the immigrants who passed through these buildings. In three floors of self-guided exhibit and audio displays, it uses restored areas, educational facilities, and more than 2,000 artifacts—personal papers, jewelry, religious articles, and clothing—to tell tales of countless weary travelers. Enter through the first-floor Baggage Room, through piles of "all their worldly possessions," and view the video, which will help you plan your tour of the main building and the American Immigrant Wall of Honor.

Young visitors will be fascinated with the Baggage Room and piles of precious items that hardly mirror the most prized possessions of children today. Do you feel a teachable

EATS FOR KIDS You can eat at the convenient **food court** here, serving American and ethnic foods, or call ahead and order a boxed lunch to pick up on the day of your visit. Lunches run $10–$16 and include a deli sandwich, chips, cookies, and a drink. (212/344–0996, www.ellisretail@aramark.com).

MAKE THE MOST OF YOUR TIME A self-guided program booklet for kids 7 to 12 gives them the opportunity to learn about Ellis Island and become a Junior Park Ranger. This booklet walks you through the historic Immigration Station and focuses on the importance of protecting and preserving this National Monument. The guide takes about an hour to complete and is available at the Ellis Island Information Desk. This nifty resource is the perfect first-time tour for families with young kids. While this is an onsite activity, kids can also participate in the National Park Service's Junior Ranger Program by becoming a Webranger, by visiting www.nps.gov/webrangers.

 New York Harbor

 Free; ferry fees $11.50 ages 13 and up, $4.50 children 4–12

Daily 9–5, ferry daily every 30 min; open daily except December 25

Tickets and monument passes (877-LADY TIX, www.statuecruises.com); Ellis Island information (212/363-3200, www.nps.gov)

 7 and up

moment coming on? The film footage may appeal more to older children 9 and up, who are most likely to sit for the award-winning footage documenting the Ellis Island experience. The outdoor Wall of Honor is a place your children can stroll or run, or explore the promenade. 600,000 immigrants' names are inscribed in steel along the wall and families can pay to have a name added. Recognizable names include Miles Standish, Priscilla Alden, and Irving Berlin. It's the largest memorial wall of names in the world.

The Peopling of America has 11 graphic displays chronicling four centuries of immigration. View the changing exhibits on the first floor before ascending to the Registry Room of the Great Hall. The hall, where immigrants were questioned and either granted or denied entry, has been restored. The cavernous space with soaring tiled arches seems to echo with the sounds of those hopeful souls.

If you like this sight you may also like the Statue of Liberty (#4).

KEEP IN MIND The ferry sails from Battery Park, South Ferry, at Manhattan's southern tip, and includes a visit to the Statue of Liberty (#4). The trip takes 15 minutes to Liberty Island, 15 minutes from there to Ellis Island, and 15 minutes back to Battery Park. It's good to catch the first boat in the morning to avoid long lines, unavoidable during the busiest times—weekends year-round and every day in summer.

EMPIRE STATE BUILDING

One of the most-recognized and most-photographed buildings in the world, the art deco Empire State Building has graced the New York skyline since 1931. The 1,454-foot structure with a limestone and granite exterior was built in one year and 45 days for a total of $41 million. (Renovations over the last 15 years have cost an additional $100 million, more than double the original price.) Now a National Historic Landmark, it has been featured in hundreds of films viewed by millions of moviegoers. No wonder that first-time city visitors often make it their first sightseeing stop.

After you've purchased tickets on the concourse, one level below ground level, high-speed express elevators whisk you to the 86th-floor observatory in less than a minute. A temperature-controlled, glass-enclosed area offers panoramic views of the city, and you may also take in the sights from a surrounding open-air promenade. Try the on-site high-powered binoculars for a closer view. Tickets for the 102nd floor observatory are only sold at the observatory office on the second floor and are $15 in addition to your general admission price.

MAKE THE MOST OF YOUR TIME Be advised there is no coat

check or holding area in the building and no tripods, suitcases, large bags or backpacks, glass or bottles may be brought inside. Consider shelling out $7 for the audio tour. A post office, drug store, dining options, and shopping can also stretch your visit and your wallet further (there's an ATM on the second floor of the 5th Avenue lobby) while exploring. Almost needless to say, time your visit for a clear day or a cloudless night.

350 5th Ave., at 34th St.

 212/736-3100; www.esbnyc.com

 $18 adults, $16 ages 12–17, $12 children 6–11, under 5 free

 Daily 8 AM–2 AM, last elevator at 1:15 AM

3 and up

On the second floor of the building is a simulated helicopter ride and virtual reality theater called NY SKYRIDE. While it is separate from the Empire State Building, it's possible to get combination tickets to both attractions ($25.50 adults, $17.50 children). Tweens and teens will enjoy this, but it may be lost on kids under 10.

On the clearest of days you might be able to see into five states: New York, New Jersey, Pennsylvania, Connecticut, and Massachusetts.

If you like this sight you may also like the Top of the Rock Observation Deck at Rockefeller Center (50th St. between 5th and 6th Aves., tel 212/698-2000).

KEEP IN MIND
Admission is a bargain for military men and women who arrive in uniform. They're admitted free. When you arrive here prepare to stand in 3 usually long lines: the security line, the ticket line, and the elevator line, unless you purchase the Express pass (an arguable bargain at $45), which moves you to the front of each line.

EATS FOR KIDS Along with the observatory and gift shop, the 86th floor has a **snack bar.** The area in and around the Empire State building has many retail and dining destinations. Inside the building itself there's decent Mexican food at **Chipolte**, (212/695-0412) and homemade Dressen donuts (which you can watch being made) at **Heartland Brewery and Rotisserie** (212/563-3433). The chicken's not half bad either! Got your sights set on pie in the sky? Try the ravioli pie or rigatoni pie at **Rosa's Pizza** (126 W. 32nd St., tel. 212/290-2315), right inside the Empire State Building.

F.A.O. SCHWARZ

47

It's not unusual, especially around the holidays, for lines to stream out the doors and down the sidewalk next to F.A.O. Schwarz, back in form after a hiatus and on its way to once again becoming the city's—if not the world's—quintessential toy store. From mid-October to the end of December an average of 75,000 shoppers a day visit this 50,000 square foot toy mecca. During December, 2.25 million people shop here, and an estimated 300,000 people per day view the holiday window displays.

Ride in the giant robot elevator for an overview of the store's three floors. The first-floor stuffed animal collection is one of the most extensive anywhere, with many in the menagerie twice as big as your young shoppers. Classic toys are also on the first floor. You may not be able to save dessert for last here, as the Ice Cream Parlor is on the first floor, inviting and delighting young and old with the "marble" counter, and decadent delicacies.

EATS FOR KIDS For scrumptious desserts, salad bar, sandwiches, and antipasto, take a trip to **Mangia** (50 W. 57th St., tel. 212/582–5882). For a frightfully fun meal, eat at **Jekyll & Hyde** (1409 6th Ave., tel. 212/541–9505), where special effects are more special than the cuisine.

MAKE THE MOST OF YOUR TIME To avoid crowds shop weekdays before lunch, or during the early afternoon and on weekends, the earlier the better. Rather than carry your purchases around the city, consider shipping them home. If you're staying in the city, the store will deliver your packages to your Manhattan hotel.

767 5th Ave., at 58th St.

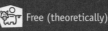 Free (theoretically)

 M–W 10–7, Th–Sa 10–8, Su 11–6

212/644–9400; www.fao.com

1 and up

Remember Tom Hanks dancing on the giant floor keyboard in the movie *Big*? Well, it's here, at the top of the escalator on the second floor. Visitors line up to do a (shoeless) turn on the ivories. A replica of the piano is available to take home for $250,000 (a smaller piano dance mat retails for a more modest $60).

The second floor is also doll heaven. The Barbie area has everything under the sun. Another hot ticket on the second floor is what's billed as the only Harry Potter shop in the United States and, perhaps more novel (pardon the pun) is the LEGO shop, with some mind-blowing, larger-than-life sculptures. The lower level features a Book Nook and child-friendly wide aisles for strollers, as well as a nursing area. Call ahead for free story hours with the Fairy Princess.

If you like this site, you may also like the Sony Wonder Technology Lab (#8).

KEEP IN MIND Compare prices beforehand, so you know exactly how much you're overpaying. There are no great bargains to be had here price-wise, but you can't beat the selection. Browse the Web site ahead of time, and discuss spending limits. With an older child, you might even use a store visit as a lesson in basic economics. Compare prices together, and decide how best to be savvy shoppers. But since most youngsters are acquisitive as well as inquisitive, it's realistic to expect that you'll leave the store with a toy (or two) in tow.

FEDERAL HALL NATIONAL MEMORIAL

B uilt in 1703 to serve as New York's city hall, Federal Hall became the first Capitol of the United States under the Constitution and is often considered the birthplace of our nation's government. On its steps stands a statue of George Washington created in 1883 by a relative of his, sculptor John Quincy Adams Ward. Washington was sworn in as the country's first president on this very site in 1789.

The original building was demolished in 1812, and the present structure was completed in 1842 and served as a U.S. customs house. This Greek Revival building was modeled after the Parthenon, another symbol of democracy. Notice the impressive exterior's 16 Doric columns constructed of Tuckahoe marble, quarried in nearby Westchester County. Each column comprises five separate pieces, each weighing 10–12 tons.

Begin your visit with an eight-minute animated video on the history of majestic Federal Hall, from the trial of Peter Zenger to the inauguration of George Washington. An exhibit

MAKE THE MOST OF YOUR TIME Free guided tours cover the history of the buildings and interpretations of memorabilia and displays. Ranger-led talks describing this historic site are held on the hour from 10 to 4. It's like a social studies textbook come to life. The Information Center at Federal Hall houses hundreds of pictures of historic lower Manhattan with self-guided theme walking tour brochures of other nearby national parks, as well as neighboring museums and restaurants. Kids can also take part in the Junior Ranger program here and get a packet of goodies, including crossword puzzles, word searches, and even a Junior Ranger badge.

26 Wall St.

Free

M–F 9–5

212/825–6888; www.nps.gov/feha

 7 and up

on the Zenger trial, a milestone in the establishment of freedom of the press, also includes an antique printing press. Can you imagine printing anything longer than a page on such a primitive press? Other key events that took place in the original building include the Stamp Act Congress of 1765, meetings of the Continental Congress, the enactment of the Northwest Ordinance, the adoption of the Bill of Rights, and the first meeting of the Congress of the United States.

Models of the original structure as City Hall and exhibits about the city and the Wall Street area are interesting, too. Look for historical memorabilia such as the bible used to swear in President Washington. The bible is sometimes used for public ceremonies, so call ahead if you want to be sure it's on display.

If you like this sight you may also like Fraunces Tavern Museum (#44).

EATS FOR KIDS **Burritoville** (20 John St., tel. 212/766–2020) serves cheap, healthy, and hefty burritos. **Cosi Sandwich Bar** (55 Broad St., tel. 212/344–5000) delights with tasty sandwiches and salads. For a quick inexpensive sit-down lunch, tasty Cuban rice and beans and take-out visit **Sophie's Restaurant** (73 New St., tel. 212/809–7755). No eating is permitted at Federal Hall.

KEEP IN MIND When Federal Hall was a customs house (1842–62), millions in gold and silver were stored in basement vaults. No money—only exhibits—remain. Though people think of customs today mainly as a watchdog that prevents smuggling, in colonial times it collected large fees from merchant vessels. In fact these fees were so big that they paid for setting up the new U.S. government; creating a navy; planning and building Washington, D.C.; constructing the military academy at West Point; and reducing the national debt to zero in 1835.

FORBES MAGAZINE GALLERIES

45

The Forbes Magazine Galleries showcase changing exhibitions from the magazine's collection of paintings, photographs, and autographs, but the big draw for kids is the personal collection of the late publisher Malcolm Forbes, on the ground floor, which includes toys and games and other unusual and sparkling items.

Young visitors should head straight to the Toy Galleries, which include more than 500 tin, cast iron, and paper lithograph toy boats made between the 1870s and the 1950s. An army of 10,000 toy soldiers engaged in elaborate displays is also here to capture their imaginations. Where else could you meet Alexander the Great, George Washington, William Tell, Buffalo Bill, or GI Joe all in the same place on the same day? A special concave viewing window lets children enter the whimsical childhood room depicted in Robert Louis Stevenson's poem, "The Land of Counterpane." Also ongoing here is a display of original handcrafted versions of the board game Monopoly and the game that inspired it, the Landlord's Game. A 1913 English version called the Br'er Fox an' Br'er Rabbit game is also exhibited. But Forbes's

EATS FOR KIDS For home-style cooking and so much more visit **Chat 'n Chew** (10 E. 16th St., tel. 212/243–1616). It's a sweetshop. It's a café. It's a dessert destination. It's **Max Brenner: Chocolate by the Baldman** (841 Broadway, tel. 212/388–0030).

MAKE THE MOST OF YOUR TIME Strollers are not permitted in the galleries and photography is forbidden. For children (and adults) truly smitten by what they see, here are a few publications to check out: *Forbes Galleries* covers collection highlights and has an introduction from the collector himself. *A Lifetime of Collecting* is Forbes's autobiography, containing 572 photographs showcasing many of his treasures. *Toy Boats* offers a pictorial history of the boats in the Forbes collection and *Toy Soldiers* highlights a century of international miniatures.

Forbes Building,
62 5th Ave., at 12th St.

 Free

 212/206-5548;
www/forbesgalleries.com

T–W and F–Sa 10–4,
Th group tour only

4 and up

noted collection goes far beyond toys to also include historical documents and memorabilia. Older children may be interested in the exhibits featured in the Lobby Gallery, the Jewelry Gallery, and the Picture Gallery. Check the Web site for descriptions of these changing exhibitions.

If your youngsters find history dull, they might find the trophies, medals, and awards in the Mortality of Immortality exhibit shinier and more interesting. As Forbes wrote, "The trophy memorabilia are humbling reminders that objects marking great occasions or victories cannot stop the march of time and that, as the pharaohs learned, you can't take the stuff with you." These collections can't help but make you think that, wealth and power notwithstanding, Forbes had a lot of kid in him.

If you like this sight you may also like the New-York Historical Society (#22).

KEEP IN MIND How many parents are now harboring ancient Beanie Baby collections? How many parents and grandparents have spent hours tracking down Smurfs, Barbies, Ninja Turtles, baseball trading cards, Pokemon cards, and POGs? (remember them?). There's a message in these galleries: When in doubt . . . don't throw it out.

FRAUNCES TAVERN MUSEUM

The fact that this museum is open on July 4 and Washington's birthday (though closed on other holidays) should immediately tell you something about it. Fraunces Tavern—a large brick house built by Stephen Delancey in 1719 on the city's first landfill—was a meeting place for the Sons of Liberty and best known as the site where George Washington said farewell to his loyal officers at the Revolution's end. It's the oldest surviving building in Manhattan and shares three centuries of city history, including the Colonial, Revolutionary, and early republic periods. A focal point for history buffs and children 10 and up is the exhibit "If These Walls Could Talk."

The building got its name from tavern-keeper Samuel Fraunces, Washington's steward and one of the Colonial era's most prominent black New Yorkers. Colonial governor George Clinton threw a huge gala here on Evacuation Day, when the last British soldiers left American soil at the end of the Revolutionary War. The tavern building was also where the departments of War, State, and Treasury were housed when New York was the first capital of the United States.

EATS FOR KIDS Except for the price, which is more expensive than the neighborhood's many delis, coffee shops, and sandwich places, not to mention the 18th century, **Fraunces Tavern** (tel. 212/968–1776), part of the complex that includes the museum, is the place to go back in time to dine. The best bet is the prix-fixe menu ($22), which includes appetizer, entrée, and a delicious dessert. The bar has a slightly less expensive menu with hamburgers and other kid-friendly food. The huge Revolutionary War mural should interest most young diners. The tavern is open for lunch and dinner Monday–Saturday and they offer takeout! Reservations are encouraged.

54 Pearl St.

 212/425-1778

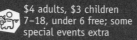 $4 adults, $3 children 7–18, under 6 free; some special events extra

T–F 12–5, Sa 10–5

6 and up

Middle schoolers and high schoolers will enjoy the artifacts, paintings, drawings, documents, and furniture found in the period rooms such as the Long Room, site of Washington's famous farewell address and now a re-created 18th-century public tavern room. Children may be delighted or dismayed to see a lock of Washington's hair and one of his false teeth. A panel from his inaugural coach is also here along with a large wooden water pipe. A Flash of Color: Early American Flags and Standards includes 200 regimental flags from the Revolution, flags of French troops, and naval banners.

If possible schedule your visit on the first Saturday of each month when family workshops, free with admission, offer hands-on activities reflecting 18th-century life.

If you like this sight you may also like the South Street Seaport Museum (#7).

KEEP IN MIND
Walking tours, tea parties, 18th-century music and dance programs, and evening and lunchtime lectures are just some of the public programs held at the Fraunces Tavern Museum. But it's a good idea to call the museum's recorded information line ahead of time to determine which of the up-coming programs are appropriate for the ages in your family.

MAKE THE MOST OF YOUR TIME Visiting the Fraunces Tavern Museum and enjoying a meal in the Tavern can be enough for one day with little ones, but if you're looking to lengthen your day trip, you're close to the South Street Seaport, the ferry for the Statue of Liberty and Ellis Island, as well as the New York City Fire Museum and the Lower East Side Tenement Museum.

HISTORIC RICHMOND TOWN

In the heart of Staten Island, this beautiful 100-acre park may be one of the city's best-kept secrets. The village contains 28 preserved historic buildings and a few reconstructions that interpret three centuries of Staten Island's daily life and culture. Ten buildings are on their original sites; the others were moved from elsewhere on Staten Island. Currently 12 buildings are open to the public.

The village of Richmond began in the 1690s as a crossroads settlement among scattered farms. The Congregation of the Reformed Dutch Church built a combined religious meeting house, school, and residence for its lay minister and teacher around 1695. By 1730, Richmond had become the island's principal political center, and throughout the 18th century the village continued to increase in importance, acquiring a jail, courthouse, churches, taverns, and shops.

Few barricades separate visitors from the places where people once worked and lived. Each room, whether equipped with the tools of a trade or filled with the aroma of

KEEP IN MIND A new exhibition slated for 2008 and 2009 explores the history of American family life. Children's furniture, high chairs, cradles and carriages dating back to the 18th century may catch your children's eye as they compare bibs, bottles, and baby clothes.

MAKE THE MOST OF YOUR TIME If you're planning a visit, call to see if any special family events (reservations required for some) are coming up. A sampling includes Halloween in Richmond Town, Old Home Day/Harvest Festival, Christmas in Richmond Town, an Independence Day Celebration, Pumpkin Picking at the Decker Farm, and a historic military Encampment Weekend. All of these happenings are a treat for young and old, but youngsters 4 to 12 will be especially entertained. The Richmond County Fair also takes place here, combining traditional events with modern pastimes, a great way to spend the day with tots to teens.

441 Clarke Ave., Staten Island

 718/351-1611;
www.historicrichmondtown.org,
www.richmondcountyfair.org

 $5 adults, $3.50 children
6-18 and students; some
special events extra

 July–Aug, W–Sa 10–5, Su 1–5;
Sept–June, W–Su 1–5

 All ages

something baking, will take you back in time. Begin at the 1837 Third County Courthouse Visitor Center to get a visitor's guide to points of interest. The Historical Museum is in the former County Clerk's Office. The Voorlezer's House is Richmond's oldest building on its original site as well as the country's oldest elementary schoolhouse. Visitors of all ages are always intrigued by the outhouse and most marvel at demonstrations of printing, tinsmithing, and other trades performed by artisans in period costumes. Children 4 to 10 will most enjoy these hands-on activities and may be asked to lend a hand in the Basketmaker's House or help with another chore. When demonstrations aren't happening, a guide is present to give an overview of the setting and answer questions. And more than 200 of the best-loved toys from the 1840s to the present are displayed in the Historical Museum in TOYS!

If you like this sight you may also like Fraunces Tavern Museum (#44).

EATS FOR KIDS A picnic area just east of the visitor center is the perfect spot to bring your own refreshments and enjoy them under a shady tree. **Golden Dove** (3281 Richmond Ave., tel. 718 967–1900) has diner fare at reasonable prices. **Peking Taste Restaurant** (3279 Richmond Ave., tel. 718/948–4445) offers traditional Asian favorites in a family-friendly atmosphere. Try **Euro Pizza** (2171 Richmond Ave., tel. 718/966–7518) for pizza and pasta.

JEWISH MUSEUM

Nestled in the elegant 1908 Warburg Mansion on the city's Museum Mile, the Jewish Museum chronicles 4,000 years of Jewish culture through art. The permanent exhibition, "Culture and Continuity, the Jewish Journey," takes up two floors and includes 800 works covering art, archaeology, ceremonial objects, video, photography, television excerpts, and interactive media. A family audio guide (free), for ages 5 and up, and an activity book ($18 in the museum's shop) guide you through this core exhibit. Young visitors tend to find the re-creation of an ancient synagogue of interest, whereas older children enjoy television and radio programs from the museum's broadcast archive as well as a film on Jewish rituals in a gallery filled with ceremonial objects. Monday through Thursday, daily 45-minute tours of the special and permanent exhibitions are given free with admission.

Draw and Discover classes are offered for children 5–12. Art classes for tweens 11–14 are also available. Teen programs including video workshops, an internship program, a High School Film Fest and SummerArts are also of special interest to older children. The fourth-floor Children's Gallery has changing exhibitions for young visitors, and each always

EATS FOR KIDS Lunch, snacks, and a light dinner are available at the museum's glatt (that means ultimate) kosher **Cafe Weissman.** You can't go wrong at the **Barking Dog Luncheonette** (1678 3rd Ave., tel. 212/831–1800), offering breakfast, lunch, dinner, brunch, and a drinking fountain just for canines, in case you've brought your pooch (though it's not allowed inside). Try a burger on focaccia bread, the marvelous meat loaf, or a yogurt sundae with granola topping. For home style, wholesome food, not to mention a great Sunday brunch, try **Sarabeth's** (Hotel Wales, 1295 Madison Ave., tel. 212/410–7335). Sample the raisin scones, sticky buns, or pumpkin waffles.

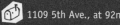 1109 5th Ave., at 92nd St.

212/423-3200;
www.thejewishmuseum.org

 $12 adults, $7.50
students 13 and up,
under 12 free, Sa free

 Sa–W 11–5:45, Th 11–9, F closed

2 and up

includes interactive components for inquiring minds and busy hands. Adventures in Archaeology invites young visitors to discover methods and techniques that study the past. Family fun is on the schedule every Sunday when you can drop into the Family Activity Center and participate in hands-on crafts workshops. You can also listen to a free ½-hour story time for ages 2 to 5. Family tours are offered the second Sunday of the month along with kids concerts and musical theater presentations. The museum's first two floors contain temporary exhibits that are more often of interest to adults.

Other family programs include Stories and Songs for kids 4–7, Art Adventures, and holiday craft and activity workshops. Most events are free.

If you like this site you may also like the Jewish Children's Museum (792 Eastern Parkway, tel. 718/467–0600).

KEEP IN MIND
If your family finds it hard to come up with something to do on Christmas, consider coming here. Unless December 25 falls on a Saturday, the museum hosts a special Family Day with a huge array of family activities, including a colossal art workshop in the auditorium, live music, and children's video screenings.

MAKE THE MOST OF YOUR TIME Bring a printout of
the Museum's Web page to the admissions desk to get half-off one admission. Take advantage of the free family audio guide; sign language interpreted tours and specialized tours for the blind and partially sighted are also offered. Be on the lookout for Ari (that means "lion" in Hebrew) throughout the museum. Ari's picture marks fun experiences of particular interest to young museum visitors.

JONES BEACH STATE PARK

4

New York State's most renowned state park opened in 1929 and hosted 1½ million visitors its first year. Sunday traffic jams on the (then) Wantagh Causeway started soon after, and not much has changed since. Today the Wantagh Parkway still jams up on weekends as families flock to the beach's eight Atlantic Ocean bathing areas and Zachs Bay from points even farther than New York City, 33 miles away.

As you approach the beach by bus or by car, be on the lookout for the Jones Beach Tower, a familiar landmark modeled after the campanile of St. Mark's Cathedral in Venice. It's 231 feet high and made of brick and stone, housing a 315,000-gallon water tank. Believe it or not, this tower provides all the water for the entire park. So if you're about to ask, "Are we there yet?" just look for the Jones Beach Tower.

The park comprises 2,413 acres with 6½ miles of beach frontage and ½ mile of bay frontage. East and West bathhouses have Olympic-size pools, diving areas, wading pools, lockers,

KEEP IN MIND To reach the beach by train, take the LIRR to Freeport or Wantagh, where buses (tel. 516/228–4000) connect to the beach. By car, take the Northern or Southern state parkways or LIE east to the Meadowbrook or Wantagh parkways south to the park.

MAKE THE MOST OF YOUR TIME If you have a lot of gear to haul, you may want to head to Field 6. It's the closest distance from the parking lot to the sand—and it does fill up first. All other lots are on the north side of Ocean Parkway. Another strategy is to arrive in late afternoon around 4 when many cars have left the parking lot: avoid the harmful rays of the midday sun, enjoy a less crowded beach-front, and stay for dinner.

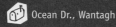
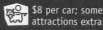

and showers. A 2-mile boardwalk is popular with young and old, and there are shuffleboard courts, paddle tennis, softball fields, volleyball, miniature golf, a fitness walk, basketball, dancing nightly at the band shell, concerts, and special events. Surfing is permitted at the West End 2 area from the Monday after Thanksgiving through Labor Day, so surfer-free families may wish to avoid this crowd. With young children, infants to age 6, head to Zachs Bay, a gentle bathing area.

Another draw is The Nikon at Jones Beach Theatre, at Zachs Bay, Field 5, which offers a sensational summer concert schedule with seating for 14,000. A 104-foot-wide stage with a 76-foot revolving center has an underwater tunnel leading from shore to stage. Parents will relive their concert days and enjoy bringing their tweens and teens here.

If you like this sight you may also like the beach at Rye Playland (#10).

EATS FOR KIDS Part of the fun of the beach is crunching that sand in your peanut butter sandwich. But for those who choose not to cart a 10-ton cooler across the beach, **refreshment stands** dispense drinks, cool desserts, hot dogs, and snacks. National chains, including **Nathan's** (nine locations), **Pizza Hut,** and **Friendly's** (nine locations including an ice-cream parlor–restaurant above the West Bathhouse), can be found all along the boardwalk and at other concessions. Barbecue and picnic areas are also abundant.

KUPFERBERG CENTER PERFORMANCES

Kupferberg Center Performances, (formerly Colden Center), part of the Kupferberg Center for the Performing Arts at Queens College, has been presenting world-class performing artists in the fields of music, dance, theater, jazz, popular entertainment, children's and family programming, and arts education since 1961. Performances are held at the Samuel J. and Ethel LeFrak Concert Hall, a 489-seat state-of-the-art recital hall with recording studio, or the Colden Auditorium, which seats 2,124 and has excellent acoustics and sight lines.

Family Theatre performances might include such universal favorites as the *Nutcracker* ballet, Plaza Theatrical's *The Emperor's New Clothes*, the annual lunar New Year celebration, the Moscow Circus, or a young people's concert. Many events are ideal for all ages; others have age recommendations.

MAKE THE MOST OF YOUR TIME
There's lots to see and do on campus besides performances. The Godwin-Ternbach Museum's collection comprises more than 3,500 artworks, and four major exhibitions are mounted annually. The Queens College Art Center's Benjamin S. Rosenthal Library exhibits modern and contemporary art. The Louis Armstrong Archives contain the great jazz pioneer's recordings, instruments, manuscripts, memorabilia, photographs, and scrapbooks. His home in Corona is also open to the public, with tours and special events in the Armstrong Garden.

Queens College (off Long Island Expressway between exits 23 and 24 at Reeves Ave.), Flushing, Queens

718/793–8080; www.kupferbergcenterarts.org

 Varies by event

 Performance times vary

Varies by performance

Besides the exceptional programming just for kids, selected all-age special events and individual performances in the fields of dance, music, and theater may also be of interest to your children. For example, a dance performance of Ballet Folklorico of Mexico, inspired by Amalia Hernandez's unique vision of an ancient land of many cultures, will take your child on a journey to a world where jaguars roam and lords of heaven and earth come back to life.

If you like this site you may also like a performance at Puppetworks (#15).

EATS FOR KIDS
For eastern or vegetarian fare try **Happy Buddha** (135–37 37th Ave., Flushing, tel. 718/358–0079). **Acquista Trattoria** (17801 Union Turnpike, Flushing, 718/969–1411) is a family-run Italian restaurant nearby.

KEEP IN MIND It's not too early to practice concert etiquette. Teach your teens to turn off their cell phones and do the same. Try opening candy wrappers and snacks before the lights dim and the performance begins. A sandwich bag of Cheerios can sometimes occupy a young child whose interest is waning. Encourage older concertgoers to stretch their legs and save their conversation for intermission. And remember to throw out all your trash.

LIBERTY SCIENCE CENTER

39

Liberty Science Center has reopened after spending two years renovating the interior, adding a new wing, and replacing 90% of the exhibitions. The first thing to wow your children (and you) is still the 700-pound Hoberman Sphere, which expands and contracts repeatedly in the atrium. It's mesmerizing to watch it seemingly explode into the huge space. But don't linger too long, or you miss all the fun of eight major exhibition areas on the four themed floors. I Explore allows scientists 2–6 (accompanied by an adult) discover who they are, what they can do, and how their bodies work.

The first-floor Skyscraper! Achievement and Impact exhibition will captivate children 7 and up with a host of construction-related experiences and machines. Your children can walk an I-beam 18 feet off the floor, or have a blast in the Curtain Wall test, which pummels selected audience members with nor'easter forces winds and rain.

EATS FOR KIDS Check out the great views and a range of meals and snacks from soup to sandwiches, including pizza and kids meals at **Café Skylines**. Also inquire at the welcome desk if you've brought your own brown bag lunch for places indoors or outside for where to park your picnic.

MAKE THE MOST OF YOUR TIME Liberty Science Center is in the 1,000-plus acre Liberty State Park. The park has the area's largest playground, a spectacular waterfront walkway with up-close views of the Statue of Liberty and Ellis Island, and Circle Line ferries to get to them. For those who don't mind walking, take the Liberty State Park ferry to the park, walk about 15 minutes to the Science Center for a visit, then spend the rest of the day having a picnic or flying kites. Or, take the ferry to the Hudson-Bergen Light Rail and get dropped off right by the Science Center.

Liberty State Park,
Jersey City, NJ

 201/200-1000;
www.lsc.org

 $14 adults, $11.50
children 2–12; IMAX
and 3-D show extra

 Mar–Aug, daily 9–5;
Sept–Feb, T–Su 9–5

2 and up

The third-floor exhibit Communication will be of special interest to teens 13 and up, as well as those 7–12. Here, kids can make weird sounds with a mechanical voice box, leave a glowing handprint on a digital wall, and learn new phrases in language karaoke. Infection Connection includes a ride around the world in a subway car theater.

On the fourth floor kids can view three massive fish tanks, operate a virtual cargo container loader and submersible robotic device, and experiment with how rivers form and flow at a long stream table. Also here is a 20-foot fossil-studded Rock Climbing wall. Don't forget to check the schedules to see what's playing in the IMAX Dome Theater or the Digital 3D Theater, both recommended for children 6 and up.

If you like this sight you may also like the New York Hall of Science (#23).

KEEP IN MIND Liberty Science Center offers timed-ticketing on busy days with 3 sessions daily. You can stay as long as you choose after entrance until closing. See ticket FAQs at www.lsc.org. Tickets are available online and can be reserved ahead. Also as a courtesy to others, please note children under 2 are not permitted in the IMAX theater. Summer and school holidays are the busiest times here with January and September the least crowded months. (And about that Hoberman Sphere . . . buy a replica in the gift shop for the kids. It will keep them entertained for hours!)

LOWER EAST SIDE TENEMENT MUSEUM

Chronicling a variety of immigrant and migrant experiences in Manhattan's Lower East Side, this urban living-history experience comprises a series of guided tours of an 1863 tenement building (the first tenement declared a National Historic Landmark) and its neighborhood. The museum is only open through guided tours, which start at the visitor center. Video presentations tell the history of the building and neighborhood, and feature interviews with residents past and present. Children 12–18 can make valuable connections between what they've learned at school and what they see on the tour. Children 8–12 will enjoy hearing about the individual family members who lived at 97 Orchard Street. Some may also have learned about the immigrant experience at school or at home.

Of particular interest to children 5–8 is the one-hour Confino Living History Tour, which focuses on a Sephardic-Jewish family in 1916. This hands-on experience begins with a costumed guide welcoming you as if you're a newly arrived immigrant. Children can ask questions and touch objects in this apartment, unusual in a typical museum. Perhaps mom

EATS FOR KIDS Ethnic eateries abound. Have a knish or potato latkes (pancakes) at **Yonah Schimmel's Knishery** (137 E. Houston St., tel. 212/477–2858), a Lower East Side institution that began from a pushcart. For dim sum or veggie dumplings, try the **Dumpling House** (118A Eldridge St., tel. 212/625–8008). Not a lot of seating, but it's authentic and delicious. Some of the best slices are dished out at **Rosario's Pizza** (173 Orchard St., tel. 212/277–9813).

Visitors Center, 108 Orchard St., at Delancey St.; tenement, 97 Orchard St.

 Tour $17 adults, $13 students; multitour discounts

Visitor center M 11–5:30, T–Fr 11–6, Sa–Su 10:45–6; tour times vary

212/982–8420; www.tenement.org

8 and up

and dad and the kids can fox trot to the music on the wind-up Victrola. If you try hard, maybe you can imagine a child's life here in 1916. "Getting By: Immigrant Families Weathering Hard Times," is a one-hour visit to the apartments of the Gumpertz family from Germany and the Baldizzi family from Sicily. "Piecing It Together" is a one-hour tour of the apartments of the Levines, who ran a garment factory from their parlor, and the Rogarshevsky family from Lithuania. The "Neighborhood Walking Tour" is a 1½-hour stroll (probably too much for young children) through the Lower East Side. Any of these walks back in time reveal families' daily struggles to survive. In 2008, the Moore Family Apartment tour will include the Irish immigrant saga in story and song.

If you like this sight you may also like Ellis Island (#49).

MAKE THE MOST OF YOUR TIME

Nearby Seward Park has a large, safe playground and shady benches. Next door at East Broadway and Essex streets is a branch of the New York Public Library with public Internet access and occasional children's programs. Also check out **Economy Candy**, (108 Rivington St., tel. 800/352–4544) it's filled to the rafters with classic treats.

KEEP IN MIND Tour tickets are available on a first-come, first-served basis, and they sell out quickly, as groups are limited to 15. Tickets for weekday tours and programs may be purchased in advance by credit card online or by calling 866/811–4111. Call the visitor center for details about multitour discounts on advance tickets. Sunday at the museum is especially crowded. Also note the museum has no elevators, and strollers are not allowed inside. There's no stroller check, but you can leave yours at the visitor center. There are lockers for shopping bags, diaper bags, backpacks, and coats.

MADAME TUSSAUD'S WAX MUSEUM

Leave your autograph book at home, but grab your camera and get up close and personal with your favorite celebrities at Madame Tussaud's Wax Museum. Though Madame Tussaud's has been entertaining Europeans with its signature wax figures for more than 200 years, this 85,000-square-foot, five-story New York City showplace is relatively new. More than 200 uncanny lifelike wax "portraits" are featured in six theme, interactive exhibits. Must-sees here include Usher's Virtual Music Experience, where Usher greets guests as Beyonce effortlessly dances beside him. Multicolor light beams project from floor to ceiling. Toddlers to teens will want to break the light beams with body movements to trigger and mix clips of his famous songs. Your curious cooks will also want to peek in the fridge in Rachael Ray's brightly colored kitchen to see what's cooking on her television show set. Take a recipe card home or test your knowledge of this Food Network star with a quiz.

KEEP IN MIND It takes four months to create a wax figure, including 140 hours for artists to carefully insert hair strands one at a time. Many celebrities donate their clothes for their own figures. Joan Rivers even donated her favorite nail polish to make a perfect match! Once on exhibit, each wax portrait is inspected and groomed daily.

The Opening Night Party, in a baroque Italian garden, lets you mingle with the New York A-list while waiting for the latest Broadway reviews to be posted. Look for Samuel L. Jackson, John Travolta, Oprah Winfrey, Hugh Grant, Bette Midler, Meryl Streep, and

MAKE THE MOST OF YOUR TIME If you're visiting with children under 12 or extremely sensitive teens, avoid Chamber Live! Featuring *Texas Chainsaw Massacre*, *Friday the 13th*, and *Nightmare of Elm Street*. This disturbingly graphic display of three iconic horror films evokes suspense and fear and features a cast of live actors dressed as the terror masters of these films. Children, but also some teens or adults, may find this exhibit extremely alarming.

234 W. 42nd St.

 212/512–9600;
www.nycwax.com

 $29 ages 13 and up, $23 children
4–12; film $2 extra

 Open 365 days a year at 10 AM.
S–Th last ticket sold at 8 PM,
F–Sa last ticket sold at 10 PM

5 and up

Nicolas Cage, among others, sharing the latest gossip. Make J.Lo blush by whispering something sweet in her ear.

In the Gallery you can come face-to-face with American presidents and some of the world's greatest leaders. In the Ultimate Subway Series, you can throw a pitch as David Wright and Derek Jeter and fans lead the cheers.

Young moviegoers will recognize and enjoy the Pirates of the Caribbean Dead Man's Chest room, meant to replicate the famous Black Pearl Ship. Or see Superman Returns, in a giant dome theater intricately decorated like Metropolis. Kids enter through a phone booth and can pretend they're Superman as a subway car levitates in midair, inviting them to stand under and "lift" it.

If you like this sight you may also like the Sony Wonder Technology Lab (#8).

EATS FOR KIDS Hungry for a quick snack and a chance in the spotlight? Audition at Madame Tussaud's New York American Idol Café. Following your performance, hear Simon Cowell's critique, and see his eyes roll before grabbing a bite. Directly across the street, **Chevys** (243 W. 42nd St., tel. 212/302–4010) has great Tex-Mex food and an extensive menu for kids and adults that's not a lot of dough. In the same building but two doors down from the wax museum, the **42nd Street Eatery** is a food court with fare from popular chains.

MADISON SQUARE GARDEN

Sitting on top of Penn Station and spanning nearly one million square feet in the heart of New York City, this is perhaps the world's most famous arena. Generations of New Yorkers can fondly remember coming to various incarnations of "The Garden" to see a variety of sports, from boxing to basketball, as well as other types of performances. Today's Madison Square Garden traces its beginnings to the 1874 Great Roman Hippodrome, built by showman P. T. Barnum. In 1877 it was taken over by bandmaster Patrick Gilmore and renamed Gilmore's Garden. In 1879 Cornelius Vanderbilt's son, William, renamed the complex Madison Square Garden, and so its descendant—which opened in 1968 and was fully renovated in 1991—is known today.

The main arena seats 20,000 and is the spring site of performances by Ringling Bros. and Barnum & Bailey Circus. Preschoolers to teens will enjoy seeing the circus at Madison Square Garden. It's also home to the New York Knicks and New York Liberty basketball teams, New York Rangers hockey team, and events ranging from concerts to boxing bouts, and from

EATS FOR KIDS You can get a deli sandwich at **Ben's Kosher Delicatessen** (209 W. 38th St., tel. 212/398–2367) or dunk a doughnut at **Krispy Kreme** (2 Penn Plaza, 33rd St. on Amtrak level, tel. 212/947–7175). Head to Macy's and **Emack & Bolio's** (151 W. 34th St., 4th fl., tel. 212/494–5853) for ice cream and yogurt in heavenly flavors. In addition to memorabilia discounts, your tour ticket stub is good for 10% off weekday lunch and during Knicks, Rangers, and Liberty games at the Garden sports restaurant, **Play by Play** (4 Penn Plaza, tel. 212/465–5888). For other choices, check out Penn Station's lower concourse.

7th Ave. between 31st and 33rd sts.

 Events vary; tour $17 ages 13 and up, $12 children 12 and under

Event times vary; tour M–Su 10–3

212/465–MSG1, 212/465–5800 tours; www.thegarden.com

 Varies by event; tour 7 and up

award shows to dog shows. Your sports fans, young and old will thoroughly enjoy a basketball or hockey game here any evening or afternoon. In 1877 Gilmore's Garden played host to the first annual N.Y. Bench Show, now famous as the Westminster Kennel Club Dog Show. Various ice shows and other children's fare are offered throughout the year. The 5,600-seat WaMu Theater at Madison Square Garden also hosts children's shows.

An exciting add-on for kids 8 and up is the one-hour All Access Tour, which enables you to stand courtside on the Knicks floor, get behind the glass on the Rangers ice, and learn how the basketball court becomes a hockey rink.

If you like this site, you may also like a New York Liberty Basketball game here (#21).

MAKE THE MOST OF YOUR TIME

Visit the Walk of Fame to find names—from Elton John to Billie Jean King to Gunther Gebel-Williams—representing more than a century of memorable sports and entertainment. In 1992 the first 25 members, chosen from more than 240 nominees, were inducted. See how many famous people you can identify.

KEEP IN MIND My memories of Madison Square Garden span almost half a century. I remember seeing the circus here as a child and I have brought my three children here to see the same. As a teenager I attended concerts here and of late can report, my own teenagers have seen their share here as well. Sporting events! Forget about it! It's the best place to experience the thrill of a game. If you haven't been, it's worth the trip. If you've stayed away too long, it's time to go back and bring the kids!

METROPOLITAN MUSEUM OF ART

At two million square feet, the Met, as it's known, is the largest art museum in the Western Hemisphere. Its permanent collection houses nearly two million works of art from all over the world, including objects from the Paleolithic era to modern times. If you spent a minute looking at each object here without taking a break, it would take more than four years to see it all. So start small. Pick two to four areas to explore and plan to return. Free lectures and walking tours covering various parts of the museum are offered, and the museum's Family Audio Guide, ideal for children 6–12, includes commentary about more than 100 works of art.

Certain areas of the Met are particularly fascinating to children, and yours will no doubt enjoy the Costume Institute, on the ground floor, as well as the musical instruments, on the second floor by the American Wing's courtyard. Sports fans check out the baseball cards in the first-floor American Wing side gallery. Be sure to visit the popular Arms and Armor Hall, on the first floor, and the Egyptian Galleries. Ruminate among the ruins

KEEP IN MIND Strollers are permitted here, but you can borrow back carriers for free at the 81st Street entrance. On Sunday, Discoveries, (tel. 212/879–3561) is a workshop for children and adults with developmental or learning disabilities.

MAKE THE MOST OF YOUR TIME After your visit, take a quick walk to the Ancient Playground at E. 84th St. in neighboring Central Park. Children will enjoy the pyramids here that reflect the theme of the Museum's Egyptian Temple of Dendur, which you can see from the playground through the glass wall across the street. If you're truly ambitious you can visit the Cloisters at Fort Tryon Park (tel. 212/923–3700) as your admission donation covers both the Met and the Cloisters on the same day. This branch of the museum is devoted to the art and architecture of medieval Europe and will probably not interest most children under 13.

5th Ave. and 82nd St.

 Suggested donation
$20 ages 12 and up,
$10 students, under 12 free

 T–Th and Su 9:30–5:30, F–Sa 9:30–9

 212/535–7710;
www.metmuseum.org

 4 and up

and the mummies and the Temple of Dendur, a real Egyptian temple moved here to save it from destruction. It's one of the most looked-at works of art in the museum.

On weekends and holiday Mondays, visitors are welcomed by special family greeters, easily spotted in bright red aprons in the Great Hall. Ask them about Holiday Monday family programs for children 5–12. Pick up a self-conducting activity guide and museum hunts at the Uris information desk, as well as a listing of recommended art-related programs offered free for children and accompanying adults. Weekend programs for various ages are offered throughout the year and include Hello Met (for ages 5–12), Art Evenings for Families (for ages 6–12), Start with Art at the Met (for ages 3–7), Look Again (for ages 5–12), and Art Mornings for Families (ages 5–12).

If you like this site you may also like the Museum of Modern Art (#34).

EATS FOR KIDS All museum restaurants, including the **American Wing Café** and **Great Hall Balcony Bar,** welcome children, but the self-serve **cafeteria** is especially family-friendly. It has booster seats, high chairs, and special meals for kids 12 and under ($4.95) that come with fruit and milk or juice in a cool 3-D tray that looks like a New York taxi. The **Petrie Court Café**, a European-style waiter-service café takes reservations for dinner (tel. 212/570–3974). For a light bite, savor the food and the views of the **Roof Garden Café** (May–Oct).

MUSEUM OF MODERN ART

Nicknamed MoMA, this museum was the world's first dedicated to the education and enjoyment of modern art. Today it maintains the world's foremost collection of modern and contemporary art: more than 150,000 paintings, sculptures, drawings, prints, photographs, architectural models and drawings, and design objects.

From various vantage points inside the museum, you can enjoy the stunning views of the Abby Aldrich Rockefeller Sculpture Garden (considered by some to be the museum's most distinctive feature) with outdoor modern sculpture, seasonal plantings, and planting pools. At any point in your visit, children (young and older) will enjoy roaming, running, or ruminating here. Inside the museum, look for Ford Family Activity Guides, free brochures distributed throughout the museum that offer creative activities than engage young viewers with the art on display. You can also listen to MoMA Audio-Modern Kids. This audio tour is designed for families with young children. The Red Studio Audio Program was developed by teens for teens touring the Museum.

MAKE THE MOST OF YOUR TIME
Strollers are allowed here, but not on the escalators. Weekdays are less crowded with the morning most optimal for a visit with children. Before or after your visit with teens, explore the Red Studio on the museum's Web site. It tackles the issues and questions raised by teens about modern art. *Destination Modern Art* on the MoMA Web site is specially designed for kids 5–8. It's an animated intergalactic journey disguised as a cartoon and activity center just for kids. Don't forget to turn on the volume for the narration.

11 W. 53rd St.

 212/708–9400;
www.moma.org

$20 ages 17 and up, $12 students 17 and up, free for children 16 and under; "Target® Free Friday Nights" admission, 4–8 PM

W–Th and Sa–M 10:30–5:30, F 10:30–8

 4 and up

From the lobby, you can take the staircase to the second floor where you can find the 20,000-square-foot galleries devoted to contemporary art, museum exhibition space, video and media, as well as galleries for prints and illustrated books. The third floor has galleries for architecture, design, drawings, photography, and temporary exhibitions. Fourth- and fifth-floor galleries contain paintings and sculptures. Each of these galleries is devoted to one subject, period, artist, or set of artists. The expansive skylighted spaces of the sixth floor have 18-foot ceilings and more temporary exhibits. The lower level is home to the two refurbished Roy and Niuta Titus theaters. Innovative and creative family programs and gallery talks are offered throughout the year and often do not require preregistration.

If you like this sight you may also like the Metropolitan Museum of Art (#35).

EATS FOR KIDS
The **Modern,** a fine-dining restaurant on the first floor, may not be your first choice with kids, but two tasty and tasteful cafés, **Cafe 2** (on the second floor) and **Terrace 5** (on the fifth), just might be. Café 2 features a children's menu and has high chairs. For scrumptious desserts, salad bar, sandwiches, and antipasto eat at **Mangia** (50 W. 57th St., tel. 212/582–5882).

KEEP IN MIND You can arrange a private tour of the Museum for your family by contacting group services by e-mail at *groupservices@moma.org* or by calling 212/708–9685. For a schedule of film and media programs and to determine if they're appropriate for children, call the museum or check the Web site. Family programs and gallery talks change periodically. Call Family Programs (tel. 212/708–9805) for information on activities and events for kids.

MUSEUM OF THE CITY OF NEW YORK

33

Where in the world can you find special exhibits that might feature seats from the original Yankee Stadium, a 1980 Checker cab, a piece of the old mechanical Times Square news "zipper," and a giant bolt tightener used to build the Brooklyn Bridge? At the Museum of the City of New York, of course! Chronicling 400 years of life in one of the world's greatest urban centers, the museum showcases Gotham's past, present, and future in permanent collections and special exhibitions that rotate throughout the year. The museum's collection includes more than 1.5 million items relating to the changing cityscape with some 500,000 photographs documenting city history.

Since the four-story museum is too big to see in one visit, grab a floor plan and take a vote on what to visit. Youngsters are often fascinated by New York Toy Stories, which includes antique dolls and the famed Stettheimer Dollhouses with original miniatures of great 20th-century works of art. In the long-term exhibition PROTECT!, children 5–10 might be interested to learn about how fire and fire safety have shaped the Big Apple over four

EATS FOR KIDS They'll make 'em the way you like 'em at **Peter's Burger Place** (1413 Madison Ave., tel. 212/722–4400). If you'd rather make your own salad or get soup or a sandwich, head for **Shin's** (1414 Madison Ave., tel. 212/831–1754), a deli take-out joint with tables in a large room in back.

MAKE THE MOST OF YOUR TIME On some Saturdays from 12 to 1:30, the museum offers programs specially for kids. Arts and crafts, fun, games, and special events are free with museum admission. Past performances have included the Paper Bag Players, the Jewish People's Philharmonic Chorus, and the Origins Project, a musical journey through NYC. Reservations aren't necessary, but a parent or caregiver must stay during this program. The Web site provides the most up-to-date overview of special exhibitions, public programs, and events especially for children and families.

1220 5th Ave., at 103rd St.

 212/534–1672;
www.mcny.org

 Suggested donation $20 families, $9 adults, $5 students 6th grade–college

 T–Su 10–5

 4 and up

centuries. Kids can learn about the bucket brigades and see a hose carriage and pumpers that were pulled not by horses but by firefighters. The museum's collection of marine-related artifacts are assembled in a long-term exhibition called TRADE!, of interest to middle schoolers and teens, which looks at the history of the Port of New York and includes ship models, ships' figureheads and dioramas documenting New York when it was called New Amsterdam. While the Period Room Alcoves portraying domestic life from the late 17th to the early 20th centuries may not be the kids' favorite, the long-term exhibition PERFORM! includes special items related to the theater collection; it will tickle the imagination of visitors 5–15. It's a look at the always-changing comedies, dramas, and musicals of the Broadway stage. Another highlight of a visit here is the film, *Timescapes: A Multi-Media Portrait of New York,* beginning at 10:15 with a last show at 4:15. It documents more than 400 years of the city's development.

If you like this site you may also like the New-York Historical Society (#22).

KEEP IN MIND To get an in-depth look at the exhibits before you go, check out the Web site's Museum Collections Sampler, which includes pictures and information. In addition, some items and exhibits can only be seen on the Web, including New York Footnotes, a collection of 18th-century women's shoes from the costume collection. Also check out the 19th-century New York City valentine. Updated daily, the site contains a calendar of family events, too.

MUSEUM OF THE MOVING IMAGE

For any fan of film or television, this 60,000-square-foot museum is the place to see the nation's most comprehensive public collection of moving image artifacts. From Thomas Edison's Projecting Kinescope (circa 1897) to the most recent computer games, the museum has a wealth of materials from motion pictures, TV, and digital media.

The core exhibition, Behind the Screen, explores how motion pictures and TV programs are created, how they find their audiences, and how their place in our culture has evolved. A highlight for kids 5–15 is a section devoted to video games. You can play the classic arcade games Super Breakout, Space Invaders, and Steroids for free. A museum educator also demonstrates a working prototype of a Pong-like game that became the first home video game system. Thirteen interactive stations let you try to create a short animated movie, apply sound effects to famous movie scenes, and perform in front of a green screen just like a TV weatherperson.

MAKE THE MOST OF YOUR TIME

The museum offers a number of programs to enhance your visit. Movie-making exhibits are especially engaging when explained by a museum educator. Along with the free family workshops given weekends at 2:30, live demonstrations of filmmaking techniques, such as editing and animation are also featured; call ahead to reserve space. Also ask about special events, such as guest speakers. Each year an array of famous actors, directors, and filmmakers make personal appearances at the museum to discuss their craft. Though these are primarily of interest to adults, some will certainly interest kids, especially teenagers.

35th Ave. and 36th St., Astoria, Queens

 718/784-0077; www.movingimage.us

 $10 adults, $5 children 5-18

W-Th 11-5, F 11-8, Sa-Su 11-6:30

5 and up

Fans, no matter how young or old, will delight in the collection of moving-image artifacts. You can view the original Yoda puppet from *The Empire Strikes Back*, a mechanical Linda Blair from *The Exorcist*, vintage TV sets, and dolls of famous movie and TV characters. Wild juxtapositions abound: you can spot a miniature skyscraper model from the 1982 sci-fi film *Blade Runner* alongside a collection of original Cosby sweaters.

A popular draw for parents and kids are the Family Motion Workshops led by museum educators on weekends for guests five and up. They're free with museum admission. Learn what makes moving images move and make your own thaumatrope, a 19th-century optical toy. And don't pass up the neo-Egyptian Tut's Fever Movie Palace, an homage to 1920s movie palaces, where movie serials and shorts (free with admission) are screened daily.

If you like this site you may also like the Paley Center for Media (#18).

EATS FOR KIDS You can catch a light bite in the museum's **café**. Or, across the street from the museum, the kid-friendly **Cup** (35-01 36th St., tel. 718/937-2322), a spacious retro-style eatery, offers lunch, dinner, snacks, and desserts that are a step above the usual diner fare. More adventurous spirits can take a walk up to Broadway, between 31st and 35th streets, for a large selection of Greek restaurants and cafés. A good choice is Uncle George's (33-19 Broadway, tel. 718/626-0593), which is open 24 hours. Or follow the aroma of coffee and pastry to an outdoor table at a local pastry shop for baklava or other sweet treats.

KEEP IN MIND

In addition to letting you make an animated short, interactive stations enable you to create a flipbook starring your child or yourself. A video camera records five seconds of motion that will be distilled into 40 still images. You have the option to have them printed and turned into a book for a small fee in the Museum shop.

NATIONAL MUSEUM OF THE AMERICAN INDIAN

In 1903 New Yorker George Gustav Heye began gathering a collection of nearly one million Indian artifacts that grew into this facility. Adults find both the interior and exterior architecture of this museum as interesting as its changing exhibitions of Native American artifacts. Children tend to be intrigued by the elaborate feathers, weavings, and blankets, baskets, painted hides, Native American garments, and carvings. But whatever your family's interests, you can find plenty to see and do at this first museum of its kind dedicated to Native American culture.

Pick up a Family Guide to lead you and your children on a scavenger hunt through the museum or download the guide from the museum Web site before your visit. Children of all ages will want to start at the Welcome Wall at the entrance to hear words of welcome in hundreds of Native American languages. The Lelawi Theater shows a 13-minute (just the right length for young viewers) film about Native American life. Overhead images

KEEP IN MIND The National Museum of the American Indian also includes a research and conservation facility in Suitland, Maryland, and a museum on the National Mall in Washington, D.C.

MAKE THE MOST OF YOUR TIME The museum offers programs of interest for the entire family that are fascinating, fun, and free, including the Native Sounds Downtown concert series. In May don't miss the weekend afternoon Children's Festival. Throughout the year the museum hosts plays, storytelling, dance, museum talks, and hands-on learning activities that share the ways and worldviews of native peoples. Screenings of documentaries and films by Native American filmmakers on contemporary subjects are shown daily. Information regarding these and other activities can be found on the Web site.

George Gustav Heye Center,
1 Bowling Green

 212/514–3700; www.
AmericanIndian.si.edu

 Free

F–W 10–5, Th 10–8

5 and up

fill the 40-foot dome. Look for touch-screen computers throughout the museum inviting young hands to learn more about this rich and colorful history.

On the ground floor is the museum's newest exhibition and performance space, the Diker Pavilion for Native Arts and Cultures. Religious and cultural items are on display only with the approval of the appropriate tribes.

One of the most visited museums in New York, it occupies the first two floors of the Alexander Hamilton U.S. Custom House, a beautiful beaux arts–style building that is both a National Historic Landmark and a New York City Landmark.

If you like this sight you may also like the American Museum of Natural History (#67).

EATS FOR KIDS The Museum's **Mitsitam Café** has foods in-digenous to America like salmon and turkey. Look for buffalo burger on the menu here. (Mitsitam means "Let's Eat.") At **Burritoville** (36 Water St., tel. 212/747–1100), try the fast and delicious Tex-Mex kid-friendly burritos, que-sadillas, and tacos.

NBC STUDIOS TOUR

I t's not a sure bet that you'll see any television stars, but that possibility isn't the reason to take this hour-plus behind-the-scenes tour. The point is soaking up all the fascinating factoids and secrets of television production.

Along your journey, you'll go back in time to NBC's birth in the Golden Age of Radio. Then you can fast-forward to the days before fast-forward buttons, through landmark TV programs that your parents may have watched. Walk your way to the present through current studios, which might include those for two or three of the following: *Saturday Night Live, Late Night with Conan O'Brien, NBC Nightly News with Brian Williams*, the *Today Show*, and *Football Night in America*. You can also learn about the latest TV technology used to broadcast around the world. Because of fast-breaking events and changes in broadcast schedules, this unstaged tour varies from day to day.

Individual tickets can be purchased in advance by phone or online with a credit card, and you can also buy a combination ticket that includes a tour of Rockefeller Center (tel. 212/

MAKE THE MOST OF YOUR TIME
Before or after your tour, stop for a treat at the NBC Sweet Shop in the NBC Experience Store. This small act of dental debauchery will help keep the little ones occupied during the tour. Check out the 3-D floor map of New York City. As you walk "among" the famous landmarks, you can peruse and pick from an endless supply of colorful, eye-catching candy. If you've managed to save the sweets until the end of the tour, consume your goodies on old-fashioned park benches overlooking Rockefeller Plaza.

664–7174). Because so many groups book ahead of time, if you do choose to purchase your tickets on the day of your tour, you'll want to get here early. Tours are often sold out by early afternoon.

NBC has been offering these tours since 1933. And even if you don't rub shoulders with a present-day NBC celebrity, you might be led around by a future one: an NBC page serves as your guide, and former pages have included Ted Koppel, Willard Scott, Regis Philbin, Steve Allen, Kate Jackson, and Michael Eisner.

If you like this sight you may also like the behind-the-scenes tour at Radio City Music Hall (#12).

KEEP IN MIND There are a few things to remember about buying tickets. A discount can be had for groups of 10 or more. Check www. nbcstudiotour.com before you plan your visit to see if celebrity signings, special events, or new products will be unveiled on the day of your tour.

EATS FOR KIDS At the **Rock Center Café** (20 W. 50th St., tel. 212/332–7620), ask for a seat overlooking the skating rink in winter, the garden in spring–summer. Fans like **Mickey Mantle's** (42 Central Park S, tel. 212/688–7777) for its large portions, friendly service, oversize TV screens, and sports memorabilia. **Prime Burger** (5 E. 51st St., tel. 212/759–4729) is a best bet for burgers, shakes, and pies without pie in the sky prices.

NEW VICTORY THEATER

Reopened in 1995 as part of the theater district redevelopment, New York's oldest active theater was built in 1900 by Oscar Hammerstein. In 1902 impresario David Belasco took over the theater. Dramatic and vaudeville shows continued until 1932, when Billy Minsky opened Broadway's first burlesque in this theater. Next it was renamed the Victory, in the patriotic spirit of WWII, and ran second-run films for several decades. In the 1970s it became the block's first XXX-rated movie house. It seems emblematic of the whole Times Square face-lift that from these cultural ashes arose a phoenix for families.

Along the way, it became "reel" famous, too, making appearances in such movies as *Manhattan Murder Mystery*, the original *Shaft*, *Taxi Driver*, and, most recently, *The Siege*. Renovation began in 1994, restoring the striking facade with its monumental second-floor entry staircase and globed standing lights. Inside, the opulent domed auditorium looks almost as it did as the Belasco Theater. The two-balcony auditorium now holds 499 seats.

KEEP IN MIND VicTeens, a program for kids 11–18, lets them see a show in a teens-only section of the theater and gives them food, free stuff, and a chance to hang out with the show's castor company. How cool is that?

MAKE THE MOST OF YOUR TIME The benefits of membership include 30% discounts on tickets, priority ordering (tickets available to members before they go on sale to the general public), a member-friendly exchange policy, newsletters, various contests, and coupons for local restaurants and other establishments. Both members and the general public are invited to participate in New Vic Studios, preperformance workshops conducted by theater professionals. Each workshop highlights an activity related to the day's performance, such as juggling or dance.

 209 W. 42nd St., west of Broadway

Regular ticket prices
$12.50–$35, member ticket
prices $8.75–$24.50,
varying by performance

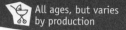 Times vary

646/223–3020;
www.newvictory.org

 All ages, but varies
by production

Recent performances have included Tony Kushner and Maurice Sendak's *Brundibar*. Dynamic dance companies, puppetry masterpieces, new vaudeville spectacles, and Tony-nominated Broadway transfers also appear here. Performance times vary from just under an hour to two hours, and shows usually run two to six weeks. The "New Vic" is wheelchair accessible, but wheelchair seats must be purchased in advance. In addition, some performances are sign-language interpreted. Booster seats for small children are also available.

If you like this site you may also like Puppetworks (#15).

EATS FOR KIDS If you're a New Vic member, take advantage of cheap eats from the Times Square locations of **Applebee's, Planet Hollywood,** or **Ben and Jerry's**. Try lunch, brunch, or dinner at **Zuni** (598 9th Ave., tel. 212/765–7626) for reasonable prices and southwestern flavors with Asian and Italian flair. For French favorites like onion soup and salade nicoise and an ample supply of butcher paper and crayons for the kids, it's **Café Un Deux Trois** (123 W. 44th St., tel. 212/354–4148).

NEW YORK AQUARIUM

By the sea, by the sea, by the beautiful sea . . ." That little ditty conjures up images of crowded, but quaint seaside attractions like Coney Island. Alongside the cotton candy and amusements, however, is this aquarium, which first welcomed visitors in 1896 at its former site in Manhattan's Battery Park and moved to this 14-acre location in 1957. It's home to more than 10,000 species of marine life, including Pacific walruses, giant sea turtles, sand-tiger sharks, and sea otters.

Don't miss the sea lion demonstrations in the 1,600-seat Aquatheater, but don't sit too close either, unless you're prepared to get splashed. Preschoolers to 10-year-olds may want to get touchy-feely with a horseshoe crab in the touch tank (May–October). Everyone will marvel at the re-creation of a rocky Pacific coast habitat for the aquarium's black-footed penguins, sea otters, and Pacific walruses. Watch them from below water inside or from above water around rocks, trees, and pools outside. Try to attend one of the feedings throughout the day.

MAKE THE MOST OF YOUR TIME
Call or visit the Web site to see what special events and children's programs might be scheduled on the day of your visit. Free public events might include a Sealife Sock Hop to the Halloween Ascarium program. Or dive right in and spend the summer as a Marine Explorer or Junior Oceanographer. In July and August, the busiest months, plan your visit at 10 AM or after 2 when the crowds thin. The least crowded months for a visit are October, November, March and April, as well as the cold days of winter.

Boardwalk at W. 8th St.,
Coney Island, Brooklyn

 718/265–FISH;
www.nyaquarium.com

 $12 ages 13 and up,
$8 children 2–12

 Daily 10–5

 All ages

In Explore the Shore, your family can stand under a 400-gallon tidal wave that crashes every 30 seconds. A Plexiglas hood keeps you dry, but the power of the sea may leave you breathless. Hands-on exhibits, interactive videos, games, and marine tanks teach about the ecology of the oceans and marshlands. Preteens to teens will want to check out the cool state-of-the-art wave machines.

From April through October, children who make the 36-inch height restriction (as well as those who don't) will clamor to take the New York Aquarium's Deep Sea 3D Ride, a simulated expedition in a hydra submarine. For a $6 ticket, or $4 when purchased in combination with Aquarium admission, you can track a giant squid's fiercest predator, the sperm whale.

At the aquarium's newest exhibit, Alien Stingers, you can come face-to-face with mysterious sea jellies. It's a must-see for everyone in your group.

If you like this site you may also like the Bronx Zoo (#64).

KEEP IN MIND A family membership in the Wildlife Conservation Society costs only $120 and lets everyone in your family visit the aquarium and the Bronx, Central Park, Prospect Park, and Queens zoos free for a year. Quite the bargain! You also get a year's subscription to *Wildlife Conservation Magazine,* a great read and valuable supply of school report pictures and articles for kids from kindergarten to college. (Trust me: You'll want to save these issues.)

EATS FOR KIDS
Eat a packed lunch on the Oceanic Deck or near Explore the Shore, or buy from the outdoor **snack bar** or indoor **Seaside Cafe.** Try boisterous, Italian **Gargiulo's** (2911 W. 15th St., tel. 718/266–4891) or **Totonno Pizzeria Napolitano** (1524 Neptune Ave., tel. 718/372–8606). The boardwalk has fast food.

NEW YORK BOTANICAL GARDEN

This 250-acre National Historic Landmark has 48 gardens and plant collections including outstanding orchids, daylilies, flowering trees, and conifers; wetlands; ponds; a cascading waterfall; a 5-acre tract of the original forest that once covered the city; and dramatic rock outcroppings. The Enid A. Haupt Conservatory, the nation's largest Victorian glasshouse, showcases rain-forest plants, desert galleries, and numerous palm trees under glass. But the reason families visit is the Everett Children's Adventure Garden, the first indoor–outdoor museum of botany and horticulture built especially for children. Its hands-on activities, imaginative exhibits, and fanciful gardens are exciting and inviting.

Stop at the visitor center for a free map and to check activity schedules. Then head for the Boulder Maze; explore its winding trail, and climb up to look through the discovery scope at the wetlands below. Next enter Beth's Maze, and find your way around the hedges. Sit or step on the oversize lily pads of the Sun, Dirt, and Water Gallery, and watch water

MAKE THE MOST OF YOUR TIME

The botanical garden is less crowded on weekdays, except Wednesday, when admission is free. A narrated tram tour, which runs every 30 minutes, lets you explore and reboard. On a hot day for the younger set and the grandparents, it's the only way to travel; and remember to bring your umbrella stroller.

EATS FOR KIDS The indoor–outdoor **Garden Cafe** and the **Visitor Center Cafe** serve kid-oriented comfort foods. Picnic tables are at the Clay Family Picnic Pavilions, outside the Everett Children's Adventure Garden. Outside the garden in the Belmont section, also called Arthur Avenue, try one of the many pizza parlors and Italian restaurants. **Dominick's** (2335 Arthur Ave., tel. 718/733–2807) or **Emilia's** (2331 Arthur Ave., tel. 718/367–5915) have inexpensive family-style Italian fare.

200th St. and Kazimiroff
Blvd., Bronx

 718/817-8700;
www.nybg.org

 Admission to the grounds
$6 adults, $2 students, $1 children
2–12; Sa 10–12 and W free; some
attractions extra; see Web site for
combination tickets

 Apr–Oct, T–Su, 10–6; Nov–Mar,
T–Su plus Monday holidays 10–5

 1 and up

shoot up. A giant frog topiary leaping from a splashing fountain invites you to discover how plants make food, move water, and use sunlight.

In the Wonder Gallery, kids can invent a plant or wander through vine-covered tunnels, tiny bridges, and a minipond. Along the Mitsubishi Wild Wetland Trail, children can get a close-up view of this fascinating ecosystem and discover What Stinks, an interactive exhibit about how wetlands recycle plants. In the family garden, visitors can dig; investigate ponds, insects, and plants; and meet gardeners from around the world. During the winter holidays, the Holiday Train Show in the Conservatory adds to the fun.

Guided walking tours on Wednesday, Thursday, Saturday, and Sunday as well as Monday holidays are probably best suited for older children.

If you like this sight you may also like the Brooklyn Botanic Garden (#62).

KEEP IN MIND The Kids Shop in the Children's Adventure Garden is a unique resource for gardening tools, toys, and plant-related items for children. The Gift Shop in the main retail area also sells plants. Consider bringing home a "please touch" plant for your garden. Lamb's Ears, Bee Balm, Lavender, and Lemon Balm are all interesting to the touch, with the last three also aromatic when the leaves are rubbed between a child's fingers.

NEW YORK CITY FIRE MUSEUM

In a renovated three-story firehouse built in 1904, you and your family can view one of the most comprehensive collections of fire-related art and artifacts from the 18th century to the present. Large firehouse doors, the housewatch (front desk) entrance, stone floor, brass sliding pole, and hose tower remind visitors of the former home of Engine Company 30, its firefighters, rigs, and horses. The nonprofit museum operates in partnership with the New York City Fire Department, which owns the building and provides the collection.

Highlights for young children or older future firefighters include getting a picture taken in a real NYC fireman's helmet and coat. Young friends will also enjoy spotting "Chief," the firehouse canine hero tucked away in his corner. Grandparents, parents, and older children interested in fire memorabilia will all enjoy the toy and model exhibit on the second floor. Permanent and temporary exhibitions chronicle the evolution of firefighting technology beginning with the early bucket brigades. Carefully preserved hand-operated, horse-drawn, and motorized equipment; toys; models; fire engine lamps (running lights from horse-drawn

MAKE THE MOST OF YOUR TIME The building can get crowded when group tours arrive, so call ahead to see if schools are scheduled when you're planning to visit. The museum also hosts birthday parties for children 4–8, and you can get fire-theme goodies from the museum store.

278 Spring St. between
Hudson and Varick Sts.

212/691–1303;
www.nycfiremuseum.org

 Suggested donation $5 adults,
$2 students, $1 children 11
and under

T–Sa 10–5, Su 10–4

2 and up

equipment); presentation silver; oil paintings, prints, and photographs; "fire marks" (emblems on buildings denoting the brand of insurance carried); and folk art illuminate the traditions and lore of firefighting.

Preschoolers and early schoolers can learn why fires were a big problem in olden days and how bucket brigades worked. They may be fascinated by how men pulled and pumped the early fire engines and how horses and dogs helped. They may also discover how firefighting changed as New York grew from a small village to a large city. Older students may be interested in the evolution of fire alarms, in the duties of today's firefighters, and in the teamwork involved in fighting fires.

If you like this sight you may also like the New York City Police Museum (#24).

KEEP IN MIND
If you live or work in Soho, you can visit the museum for free. Simply walk in and say "I'm a neighbor" and the suggested admission will be waived.

EATS FOR KIDS Hankering for Cajun cooking and cowgirl memorabilia? Head to the **Cowgirl Hall of Fame** (519 Hudson St., tel. 212/633–1133). Bleeker Street Pizza (69 7th Ave., tel. 212/924–4466) is close and will satisfy your pizza craving in a kid-friendly setting. Just hot enough to send your taste buds blazing, visit **Chipotle** (200 Varick St., tel. 646/336–6264) for fun fare with a Mexican flair.

NEW YORK CITY OPERA TARGET® FAMILY SERIES

No need to sing the praises of opera when you can experience it with your family at Lincoln Center. New York's amazing performing arts center is filled with theaters of all shapes and sizes, playing host to every type of music imaginable, dance, film, and even the circus. Of these, opera (the center is home to both the Metropolitan and New York City operas) is perhaps the least accessible for many children, but not to worry. The New York City Opera Target® Family Series, offered by the New York City Opera education department, provide an energetic and exciting kid-oriented introduction to this musical and theatrical art form.

These one-hour interactive workshops are designed especially for families. Prior to select weekend matinee performances, City Opera staff and artists conduct hands-on activities that explore the themes, drama, and music of the afternoon's opera. Everyone is encouraged to join in the fun, which may include acting out a scene, learning a dance, examining costume design, or exploring a musical score. Four family-friendly operas are usually chosen each season. Sessions have included such operas as *Carmen*, *Hansel and Gretel*, *The*

EATS FOR KIDS **Café Vienna** (Avery Fisher Hall, tel. 212/874–4700) serves sandwiches for lunch on matinee days. Though the adult fare is fabulous at **SQC** (270 Columbus Ave., tel. 212/579–0100), the real treats are the organic baby food (tofu puree, anyone?) and the kids' menu (hot chocolate is a must). Even adults order from it.

MAKE THE MOST OF YOUR TIME If your interest has been piqued by the magic of opera, take a backstage tour of the Metropolitan Opera House (30 Lincoln Center Plaza, tel. 212/769–7020) while the Met is in season, usually September–June. Marvel at castle construction in the carpentry shop, suits of armor and Cinderella gowns in the costume shop, and big hair and bald pates at the wig-maker's shop. Peek into the rehearsal room, auditorium, dressing rooms, and cafeteria. Tours ($15 adults, $5 children 4–12), recommended for those 8 and up, are weekday afternoons and Saturday mornings. Reservations are advised for this 1½-hour tour.

New York State Theater, Lincoln Center,
62nd St. and Columbus Ave.

 $15

Sa-Su 12–1

212/870–5643; www.nycopera.com

6–12

Pirates of Penzance, and *Madame Butterfly*. Advance reservations (which can be made online at the City Opera Web site) are required for the workshops, held on the Promenade of the New York State Theater, and lunch is included. Workshop times are 11:30 AM and 12:30 PM. You may purchase a family workshop ticket individually or as part of the Target® Family Series subscription package.

If you need to brush up on your Verdi, Mozart, or Puccini, visit the New York City Opera Web site and access the Learning and Resource Centers. You can read biographies, explore an opera glossary, and locate plot descriptions so you can read the story before or after you hear the opera. And if you're wondering what to wear, pretty much anything goes these days. Some families do enjoy the occasion to dress up, but the key is comfort. Remember, the aim is for everyone to have fun.

If you like this sight you may also like Kupferberg Center Performances (#40).

KEEP IN MIND Like its bubbling, dancing fountain, Lincoln Center is overflowing with wonderful family performances, from jazz to the circus, ballet to movies. Here's just a handful: the Chamber Music Society's Meet the Music Concerts for Kids (tel. 212/875–5788), Movies for Kids (tel. 212/875–5600), and the New York City Philharmonic's Young People's Concerts (tel. 212/875–5656).

NEW YORK CITY POLICE MUSEUM

Four blocks south of the South Street Seaport, in the first police precinct station (1911) in downtown Manhattan, the New York City Police Museum gives an inside look at the dedicated men and women who serve and protect the city that never sleeps. Three floors of exhibits depict a rich history that dates back to colonial times, when "watchmen" patrolled the cobblestone streets of New Amsterdam.

Begin at the oak front desk on the first floor, used from 1931 to 1999 at the Bronx's 46th precinct. Tour the Transportation Room to find both easily identifiable and unusual methods of police transportation, from bicycle patrols to the 1972 Plymouth Fury used in such movies as *The French Connection*, *Coogan's Bluff*, and *The Seven-Ups*.

The Transit and Housing police departments are saluted on the second floor. Here, too, you'll find the most photographed museum exhibit: the jail cell. Kids 8 and up will find this exhibit the most intriguing. Notorious Criminals and Weapons of the Trade includes

MAKE THE MOST OF YOUR TIME The Hall of Heroes is the museum's most solemn room, containing the shields of every NYPD officer killed in the line of duty since the department began in 1845. In the Firearms Training Simulator (FATS), visitors 18 and older are allowed to hold a real firearm. Gripping photographs, news footage, and interviews with NYPD first-responders are part of 9.11 Remembered, a moving tribute to the courage and sacrifice of the men and women of the NYPD. These exhibits may not be suitable for your children. Parental discretion is advised when visiting these three areas of the museum. Also check the museum's Web site for monthly family programs.

100 Old Slip (between Water and South Sts.)

 212/480-3100; www.nycpolicemuseum.org

 Suggested donation $7 adults, $5 children 6–18, $15 for family of 4 or more

 T–Sa 10–5

 8 and up

mug shots and gangster weapons, such as Al Capone's machine gun. The third floor contains the Wall of Valor, the Hall of Heroes, the Firearms Training Simulator, and special exhibits.

Policing a Changed City chronicles how the job of the NYPD has changed since the September 11 attacks. It also includes an interactive demonstration of the Real Time Crime Center, where visitors can enter sample data from a crime and see how the statistics in the computer lab help identify possible "perps."

A favorite among youngsters 8–15 is to pose for pictures dressed in a police uniform or take part in a make-believe lineup, all while learning about the brave men and women who keep our communities safe.

If you like this sight you may also like the New York City Fire Museum (#26).

KEEP IN MIND Did you know that the word "cop" was first used in 1845, when police shields were made of copper? Speaking of metal and medals, the first police department Medal of Valor was designed by the famous jeweler Louis Tiffany, the son of the founder of Tiffany & Co. Its design, with a superimposed N and Y (the logo of the New York Yankees) remains the same today. Young sports fans may be interested in searching for the Yankees logo in the museum.

EATS FOR KIDS
For pub-style food try **Stone Street Tavern** (52 Stone St., tel. 212/785–5658). The miniburgers are tops at **Ulysses'** (95 Pearl St., tel. 212/482–0406). With two entrances on Pearl and Stone streets, don't miss **Adrienne's Pizza Bar** (54 Stone St., tel. 212/248–3838) for rectangle pizzas with lots of pizzazz.

NEW YORK HALL OF SCIENCE

New York City's only hands-on science and technology museum is also one of the country's best. With more than 400 interactive exhibits over 35,000 indoor square feet (not to mention 60,000 outdoor square feet in the Science Playground), the hall is, scientifically speaking, *the* place to bring the family for a day of fun and learning.

The Science Playground is the largest science playground in the Western Hemisphere *and* it just doubled in size. It's water and sand and kids just go crazy for it. All ages including adults also love the Sports Challenge area where you can ride a mechanical surfboard, test your pitching prowess, climb a rock wall, and more. The ground-level Central Pavilion contains Seeing the Light, a journey into the world of color, light and perception with more than 80 exhibits. On the lower level, middle schoolers, high schoolers, and even the youngest scientists will enjoy the Biochem Lab, the world's first hands-on lab that's open to the

MAKE THE MOST OF YOUR TIME

Students with A's in both math and science can receive a free one-year Honors Membership to the museum—just another reason to hit the books. The Hall is in Flushing Meadows–Corona Park, site of the 1939 and 1964 world's fairs. Also in the park is the Queens Zoo (#13).

EATS FOR KIDS There are no restaurants really close by, so plan to pack a lunch and find a spot in the spacious 300-seat **dining hall** overlooking the park and Science Playground. No time to make a bag lunch? You can purchase sandwiches, snacks, and beverages from **Café** once you get here. **The Lemon Ice King of Corona** is a short drive–walk from the Hall (52–02 108th St.). Television viewers may recognize this popular destination from the opening credits of the *King of Queens* television show. Enjoy your ice in a small park across the street.

47–01 111th St., Flushing Meadows–Corona Park, Flushing, Queens

 718/699-0005; www.nyscience.org

 $11 adults, $8 children 2–17; F and Su free at selected times Sept–June; Science Playground $4

July–Aug, M–F 9:30–5, Sa–Su 10–6; Sept–June, M–Th 9:30–2, F 9:30–5, Sa–Su 10–6

2 and up, Science Playground all ages

public and devoted to the chemistry of living things. You can conduct your own experiments here with step-by-step instructions and help from staff.

In the Preschool Science Place, little hands can investigate sound, color and light, simple machines, and measurement in a self-contained space apart from the bustling crowds.

Outside your kids can pretend to blast off in the Rocket Park with two real NASA rockets, plus a climb-in Mercury capsule replica.

If you like this sight you may also like the Liberty Science Center (#39).

KEEP IN MIND Sometimes touring with children of varying ages is challenging. Older children are often more likely to sign on for a day at a museum or family adventure if a friend is invited. Visiting the New York Hall of Science was the first time I invited a friend along for my oldest child, who became much more amenable to accompanying his two younger sisters and me. Upon entry, he and his buddy had some freedom to explore each floor here on their own before meeting up with mom at an agreed upon time. Cell phones (vibrating, not ringing please) make it easy to keep in contact.

NEW-YORK HISTORICAL SOCIETY

Founded in 1804, the New-York Historical Society is New York's oldest museum, predating the founding of the Metropolitan Museum of Art and the American Museum of Natural History by nearly 70 years. Today it serves as a collective memory of the heritage of New York City, the state, and our nation, exploring the connections between past events and our present-day lives. More than 1.6 million items can be found here, among them the nation's largest collection of Tiffany glasswork and 433 of the 435 original watercolors from John J. Audubon's Birds of America (1827–38). Also included in the museum collections are American folk art paintings, toys, weather vanes, George Washington's camp bed from Valley Forge and his inaugural armchair, the desk at which Clement Clark Moore wrote "A Visit From St. Nicholas" in 1822, and a chair made for Marie Antoinette's private chambers at Versailles. In all, it's home to one of the country's greatest collections of American art and historical artifacts.

Scavenger hunts and activity packs, free with admission, are available for each exhibition and include games and puzzles that will stretch kids' imaginations as they become history

EATS FOR KIDS The café at **N-YHS** has sandwiches, salads, and pastries by famed foodie Eli Zabar. For some of the city's tastiest bagels, go to **H&H Bagels** (2239 Broadway, at 80th St., tel. 212/595–8003). **EJ's Luncheonette** (447 Amsterdam Ave., between 81st and 82nd sts., tel. 212/873–3444) is a sure bet for heaping portions of kid comfort food. Try the black-and-white malt. **Sarabeth's** (423 Amsterdam Ave., between 80th and 81st sts., tel. 212/496–6280) is a crowd-pleaser, especially for brunch. Don't miss the French toast, red omelet, and delectable pumpkin muffins. Lenny's (489 Columbus Ave., tel. 212/787–9368) is full of neighborhood kids, sandwiches, and made-to-order salads.

170 Central Park West,
between 76th and 77th sts.

212/873–3400;
www.nyhistory.org

 Children under 12 free,
$6 students

 T–Su 10–6

 7 and up

detectives. Audio wands are also available, free of charge at the admissions desk, for many of the special exhibitions. For some of the audio tours, teens will find it fun to use their own cell phones to dial-in to learn more.

Older teens will enjoy some of the programs reflecting current art and historical exhibitions in the museum. Previous programs have included People of the Press, where young journalists write and produce their own TV news shows and Creative Campaigning, an introduction to issues and political campaigns.

In the Great Hall exhibits such as Presidential Treasures (from the library collection), which highlights manuscripts from American presidents, are installed on a rotating basis. The Henry Luce Center displays objects from the museum's collection.

If you like this site you might like the American Folk Art Museum (#68).

MAKE THE MOST OF YOUR TIME

Family special events include such diverse experiences as learning to build birdhouses or make birdcalls, bird-watching tours of Central Park, and experiencing drumming and Afro-Caribbean Dance or listening to talks on famous artists and historical figures.

KEEP IN MIND Next time you and the kids are touring a museum, bring along a pad and pencil or sketchbook and pastels or colored pencils for older children. Find a place to sit and let them select something that catches their eye to draw or sketch. This peaceful break in the haste to "see it all" will help them focus on observation and details and may allow the adults in your group to linger longer in a particular spot, while giving your children a brief, artful, but meaningful rest. Later, add a narrative, title, or story to their sketches, drawings, or scribbles to make special memories of their visit.

NEW YORK LIBERTY BASKETBALL

It's fast-paced, it's fun, it's family entertainment, and it's affordable. If this doesn't sound like today's professional sports to you, you haven't been to a New York Liberty game. The area's hot WNBA (Women's National Basketball Association) team brings summer basketball to Madison Square Garden.

Each season has 34 games, with half played at home at the Garden. Games usually run less than two hours. During the games look for Maddie the Mascot, a friendly overgrown dog who makes friends with the fans, leads the conga lines on the court, and leads the cheers. Named for Madison Square Garden, Maddie often signs autographs and poses for pictures in the lobby before the games. She's a real favorite with the preschool crowd. Also part of the excitement here is the 12-member dance-and-performance team, Torch Patrol. This athletic, high-energy squad of young men and women conduct fun, frenzied mayhem during time-outs, incorporating tumbling, dance, and crowd interaction.

MAKE THE MOST OF YOUR TIME

Arrive early—gates open one hour before game time—to watch the pregame shoot-around and team warm-up. Technically, no photographs are permitted, but young fans with cameras do snap shots of their favorite players before the games. Don't forget to get your souvenir team yearbook. For girls interested in getting even closer to the basketball action, New York Liberty runs a girls' summer basketball camp (tel. 212/924–4040 Ext. 106) each year.

Madison Square Garden, 7th Ave. between 31st and 33rd Sts.

 212/564–WNBA; www.nyliberty.com

 $10 and up

 June–Aug, playoffs through Sept; games 7:30 and Sa–Su at 4 PM

 5 and up

At each game, the arena's most spirited section of fans is chosen to attend a postgame autograph session with team players, so get your wave ready and make your cheer loud and clear. And don't even think about leaving your seat during halftime, or you'll miss the entertainment. When was the last time you got to see Frisbee-catching dogs or bike stunts? Don't try this at home. But do practice your hook shot and keep dribbling.

If you like this experience you may also enjoy other sporting events at Madison Square Garden (#36) or a game at Yankee Stadium (#1).

EATS FOR KIDS

A popular chain known for its family cuisine, **T.G.I. Friday's** (484 8th Ave., tel. 212/630–0307) has good burgers, sandwiches, and salads. **Chipotle** (304 W. 34th in Penn Plaza, tel. (212/268–4197) is a destination for quick, big, and delicious burritos. Check for 8 other locations around the city. Also see eateries listed for Madison Square Garden.

KEEP IN MIND Promotions take place during nearly every game. Whether it's miniball or sports-poster giveaways, mascot day, or fan appreciation T-shirt night, these special events give your kids another thrill just by walking through the turnstile and getting a free souvenir. The team also holds celebrations like Flag Day, Father's Day, and charitable game promotions like a Cheering for Children Auction and Breast Cancer Awareness Night. If you have a choice, pick a game where they're giving something away. Check the Web site for a schedule of special days and giveaways.

NEW YORK TRANSIT MUSEUM

When is a museum not an ordinary museum? When it's housed in a decommissioned 1936 subway station in downtown Brooklyn. The New York Transit Museum is a walk-up, sit-down, and touch museum that is home to 100 years of transit history and memorabilia. The collections include 19 restored subway cars dating from 1904 to 1964, as well as antique turnstiles, a working signal tower, a surface transportation room, and a variety of other transit equipment. Parents and grandparents will enjoy the nostalgia of this museum while toddlers to teens will find the collections curious and engaging.

Revolving exhibits, programs, workshops, and tours provide an insider's look at MTA bridges, tunnels, subways, buses, and commuter railroads. You and your children can watch a film clip about the age of Els (elevated trains) before they fade into history. Take the A Train or catch all the trains you missed in an exhibit of full-size classic wooden cars and their modern counterparts. Or see a sign of the times in a display of nearly 200 examples of subway signage: in porcelain enamel, cast iron, brass, wood, and plastic.

MAKE THE MOST OF YOUR TIME

The museum is close to the Brooklyn Children's Museum and the Aquarium. Take in the sights at two great Brooklyn attractions and enjoy lunch in between.

EATS FOR KIDS The **Armando Ristorante** (143 Montague St., tel. 718/624-7167) offers traditional Italian fare at more than fair prices. Split a pasta dish for two or for lunch or dinner, hit the **Heights Café** (84 Montague St., at Hicks St., tel. 718/625-5555). Parents find much to choose from on the eclectic American–international menu, and kids can't go wrong with a standard burger or pizza. **Makayla Restaurant** (121 Livingston, tel. 212/797-0631) offers down-home southern cooking kids and adults will savor.

Boerum Pl. and Schermerhorn St., Brooklyn Heights

 $5 adults, $3 children 3–17

 T–F 10–4, Sa–Su 12–5

 718/694-1600; www.mta.info/museum

2 and up

In 2004 the launch of the Transit Museum's education Web site, Education Station, coincided with the commemoration of the 100th anniversary of the NYC subway. An interactive portal called Community Crossing features the Subway Centennial Student Activity Depot, with student-centered educational activities. Kids 13 and up can contribute to the Memory Project, an online community site for sharing oral histories about NYC subway and bus memories. They can send artwork, write poetry or record a story or memory. Log on to the memory line to take part in this cool history lesson.

The museum also offers guided tours of different parts of the transit system. Nostalgic Train rides are also scheduled throughout the year to destinations around the city. Call ahead for reservation information and fees (tel. 718/694-1867).

If you like this sight you may also like the New York City Fire Museum (#26).

KEEP IN MIND Don't miss the museum's annual Bus Festival, in late spring or early summer. An entire block is shut to park historic buses outside, including a wooden open-top double-decker bus and a favorite, the 1949 Jackie Gleason bus, modeled after the one driven by Ralph Kramden on *The Honeymooners*. Also: Shopping for a (subway) token of your affection to give to a (nostalgic) loved one? Look no further than the Transit Museum Gallery Annex and Store. For transit-related toys, trinkets, and memorabilia, this is the place.

NY WATERWAY FERRIES

In the early 1800s, New Yorkers traveled to and from Manhattan by ferry, but as bridges and tunnels were constructed, ferries fell out of favor. Today you can experience this form of transportation on NY Waterway, one of the largest private ferry operations in the nation. NY Waterway transports more than seven million passengers into the city each year on 34 vessels covering eight ferry routes. For commuters, ferries offer a shortcut to Manhattan minus the traffic jams, tunnel and bridge tolls, and parking problems usually associated with car travel. Ferry crossings run anywhere from five to 15 minutes, with frequent departures throughout the day.

Ferries aren't just for commuters, however. If your family wants to sightsee, you can take a fun-filled ride around New York Harbor on a Riverkeeper Kid's Ecology Cruise. This 90-minute entertaining, child-friendly voyage includes interactive onboard activities and multiple flat-screen monitor audio-video enhancements to teach families about the local ecology and history of the Hudson River. A portion of the ticket price is donated to Riverkeepers.

MAKE THE MOST OF YOUR TIME The best sightseeing bargain in the city is the free 20- to 30-minute ride on the Staten Island Ferry (tel. 718/390–5253) across New York Harbor. Take the older model blue-and-orange ferries, which sail higher in the water and have outside deck space, so you can enjoy views of the Manhattan skyline, the Statue of Liberty, Ellis Island, the New Jersey shore, and the Verrazano Narrows Bridge. Ferries run every 30 minutes during the day and evening and every hour after midnight and on weekend mornings.

Terminals in Manhattan
and New Jersey

800/533-3779;
www.nywaterway.com

Fares vary depending
on destinations, packages,
and tours

Schedules vary, depending on route

2 and up

Sightseeing tours around lower Manhattan include harbor cruises by day and twilight cruises providing up-close views of the Statue of Liberty, Ellis Island, and the Brooklyn Bridge. You can also take the Yankee Clipper to see the Yankees play ball. The Shades of Autumn tour includes breathtaking views of the Hudson River during the fall months. Dining and Broadway show packages are also available.

Hudson River cruises include tours of the legendary Rockefeller family estate in Pocantico Hills and historic Philipsburg Manor, a working Dutch Colonial farm; a Sleepy Hollow Cruise, including Sunnyside, the home of Washington Irving, and Philipsburg Manor; a scenic trip down the North Hudson River without stops; and a cruise to Lyndhurst, a great Gothic revival–style estate.

If you like this experience you may also like the ferry rides to Ellis Island (#49) and the Statue of Liberty (#4).

KEEP IN MIND
If you're taking a ferry to a Yankee game, why not make it extra special? Ask your parents to find out about tours of Yankee Stadium. Highlights include the dugout, press box, clubhouse, and Monument Park.

EATS FOR KIDS The **New York Milkshake Company** serves snacks onboard some ferries and also at Pier A in Battery Park and Pier 78. Try their grilled peanut butter and jelly sandwich or the hot waffle ice cream sandwich, often called the best all-weather dessert! If you're taking NY Waterway from Weehawken, New Jersey's Port Imperial Terminal, consider eating right at the marina at **Arthur's Landing** (Pershing Rd., Weehawken, NJ, tel. 201/867–0777), which has a kids' menu. Take the Waterways shuttle from the Port Imperial Terminal right to Arthur's Landing.

PALEY CENTER FOR MEDIA

Formerly the Museum of Television and Radio, the Paley Center was named for William S. Paley, a media industry pioneer. The big draw here for enthusiasts is the broadcast collection, which comprises more than 140,000 TV and radio programs and advertisements from the 1920s to the present. Catch classic Jack Benny or early Ed Sullivan shows, watch the first moon walk, Uncle Milty, *I Love Lucy* reruns, or the Beatles' first appearance on American television. After searching a computer database for the programs you want to see, you can watch them in the Console Center; many consoles can accommodate more than one viewer.

The museum also has three galleries exhibiting ever-changing art and artifacts relating to television and radio as well as theaters for the museum's screening series. Programs from the series vary with events of interest to teens like a recent David Bowie concert or episodes of *Saturday Night Live*, as well as screenings of interest to young visitors, like the work of Muppets creator Jim Henson. Adults and older teens may enjoy Super Bowl Super

KEEP IN MIND Visiting the West Coast? Drop by the Paley Center for Media in Los Angeles (465 N. Beverly Rd., Beverly Hills, tel. 301/786–1025). Become a member at either site and you can visit both for free.

MAKE THE MOST OF YOUR TIME If you're 9–13 and want to be on the radio, come for a Re-creating Radio workshop. No, you won't be the guest DJ on your favorite radio station—nothing that glamorous! Instead you can try re-creating performances and sound effects from shows of the '30s and '40s like *The Shadow*, *The Lone Ranger*, or *Superman*. This two hour workshop is limited to 20 participants and you get to take home a recording of the live broadcast you produce. Tickets ($7) must be purchased in advance by phone (tel. 212/621–6600) or in person on-site.

Showcase for commercials or America's Teenagers: Growing Up on Television. And since there's always something new going on, regular visitors return frequently to check out the latest special screenings and temporary exhibits.

She Made It, which chronicles the contributions of women in television and radio, is a unique collection of programming celebrating and preserving the legacy of great women directors, writers, producers, journalists, executives, and sportscasters in the industry.

A radio studio is also part of the center's facilities. Throughout the year, live radio broadcasts, which are open to the public, take place here. By dropping in, families can see what happens behind the scenes of a radio show.

If you like this site you may also like the Sony Wonder Technology Lab (#8).

EATS FOR KIDS For a meal on a bun, visit **Burger Heaven** (20 E. 49th St., tel. 212/755-2166; 536 Madison Ave., tel. 212/753-4214). For deli delights, pitas, wraps, and salads dig into **Digby's** (666 5th Ave., tel. 212/977-7272). For lunch, brunch, tea, or dinner, girls will delight in the **American Girl Café** (609 5th Ave., at 49th St., tel. 877/AGPLACE) on the third floor of this female-oriented retail establishment. The prix-fixe three-course menu is reasonable for adults, a little pricey for kids, and don't forget to try the warm cinnamon buns.

PROSPECT PARK

Prospect Park offers 585 acres of winding paths, rolling hills, open spaces, Brooklyn's only forest, and other great green places to stroll, picnic, fly a kite, or sit and think. Designed by the renowned team of Olmsted and Vaux, it's home to the 90-acre Long Meadow, one of the city's greatest open spaces, with spectacular views of grass, trees, and sky. Feed the ducks and spot the swans at 60-acre Prospect Lake with your little ones (Brooklyn's only freshwater lake), or explore the park's nature trails, which begin at the Prospect Park Audubon Center, with your older ones.

A 1912 carousel, in operation from April to October features 51 magnificently carved wooden horses, along with a lion, giraffe, deer, and dragon-drawn chariots. It's a sure bet for toddlers to 10-year-olds. Don't be surprised if your teens want to take a turn as well. This magnificent piece of Americana, originally installed at Coney Island, is at the Willink entrance at the intersection of Empire Boulevard and Flatbush Avenue.

MAKE THE MOST OF YOUR TIME Late October visitors should try to hit the Halloween Haunted Walk and Festival, held throughout Prospect Park the last Saturday in October from noon until 3 (a carnival, with performances, games, and treats, takes place near the Nethermead, the geographic center of the park). Prospect Park also hosts special community events, including Hawk Weekend in September, New Year's Eve fireworks, Earth Day Weekend in April, You Gotta Have Park in May, Macy's annual Fishing Contest, and the Celebrate Brooklyn! Arts Festival. It's no surprise more than eight million locals and tourists visit each year.

Eastern Pkwy. and Grand Army Plaza, Brooklyn

 718/965–8999 hotline, 718/965–8969 for permit information, 718/287–3400 Audubon Center; www.prospectpark.org

 Free; some attractions charge

 Daily sunrise–1 AM

9 mth and up

From mid-November to early March head for the Wollman Rink (not to be confused with Central Park's Wollman Memorial Rink in Manhattan) near the Lincoln Road entrance for ice-skating for the whole family. It's the only open-air rink in the borough. Skate rental and instruction are offered. Most of the rest of the year, this is the place to rent pedal boats, which seat four—a great way to take a break and a tour of the lake at the same time. Tennis, anyone? Visit the tennis center, open year-round at the Parade Ground (tel. 718/436–2500).

Check out the Audubon Center, at the Boathouse. It has hands-on exhibits and runs family programs with crafts and music Thursday–Sunday. The Boathouse also houses the electric boat *Independence,* which takes spring and summer tours of the park's waterways. Aquatic discovery and twilight cruises are also available.

If you like this sight you may also like Central Park (#57).

KEEP IN MIND
With the closing of Claremont Riding Academy, it's getting harder to find places to saddle up a horse. But look no further than Kensington Stables here with 3.5 miles of bridle paths for riders of all levels. Lessons run $30–$50 and an hour's ride is $30. (Kensington Stables, Prospect Park, tel. 718/972–4588.)

EATS FOR KIDS Circles Restaurant (192 Prospect Park W, tel. 718/499–5595) is next to the historic Pavilion Theater, once a single-screen movie house but now a multiplex. It can accommodate any size group. **Kate's Corner Snack Bar** (Wollman Rink) is open Thursday–Sunday. The **Songbird Café** (Audubon Center) is a natural place for a nosh. At **Second Helpings** (448 9th St., tel. 718/965–1925), an organic eatery and juice bar, kids can sample chicken, mac and cheese, PB&J, or grilled cheese, while adults indulge in sumptuous wraps on flat bread with homemade cumin chips. Yum! Also see the Prospect Park Zoo (#16).

PROSPECT PARK ZOO

This 12-acre zoo, completely revamped and transformed into a modern children's wildlife learning lab, is home to 82 species of animals and run by the Wildlife Conservation Society. Naturalistic habitat exhibits have replaced bars, cages, and pits, and the larger species that were part of the original menagerie of the late 1800s and early 1900s are gone.

Interactive and always fun to visit, the Animal Lifestyles building is home to air, water, and land animals in exhibits related to the center's wildlife education program. Children 8 and up will particularly be captivated by the reptiles, amphibians, fish, birds, and small mammals, as well as their environments. The centerpiece of the building is the 4,500-square-foot hamadryas baboon exhibit. Perched high on the rock cliffs by an impressive waterfall, separated from these fascinating social primates by an invisible sheet of glass, their somewhat less fascinating primate cousins (humans) feel very much a part of this exhibit. Don't be surprised if a friendly baboon approaches the glass to study you back.

KEEP IN MIND You'll find entrances to the zoo off Flatbush Avenue and near the Lefferts Historic House. Subway is the best way to reach here: take the S or Q train to the Prospect Park station or the B41, B47, or B48 bus.

MAKE THE MOST OF YOUR TIME Interactive educational—often musical—shows at the Wildlife Theater (Memorial Day–Labor Day, Thursday–Monday) are good for the whole family. On weekends at 11 and 3, Keeper Chats highlight a different animal each month, as a zookeeper shares animal facts and fun with the audience. The zoo also sponsors special community events—the Fleece Festival, Keeping up with Keepers, and Boo at the Zoo—free with admission.

450 Flatbush Ave., Prospect Park, Brooklyn

 718/399–7339; www.prospectparkzoo.org

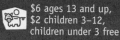 $6 ages 13 and up, $2 children 3–12, children under 3 free

Early Apr–late Oct, M–F 10–5, Sa–Su 10–5:30; late Oct–early Apr, daily 10–4:30

 All ages

More fun for kids 4 to 10 awaits in the World of Animals' 2½-acre Discovery Trail. They can burrow in Plexiglas-topped tunnels, and pop up next to a prairie dog or leapfrog across lily pads to goose nests, and pretend to hatch. In the Wallaby Walkabout, they can walk among small Australian kangaroos and other animals, and in the 2,500-foot aviary at trail's end, they can walk around free-flying African birds and climb into nests just their size.

Drawing supplies are provided in the Animals in Our Lives building. Playful meerkats, emerald tree boas, and poison dart frogs call this space home. In the barnyard, the young crowd can peek into the chicken coop or meet goats, sheep, and cows. A must-see and fun for all are the California sea lions frolicking in a rocky California coast–like environment. They are fed daily at 11:30, 2, and 4.

If you like this sight you may also like the Queens Zoo (#13).

EATS FOR KIDS Avail yourself of a **cafeteria** near the sea lion pool or bring your own lunch and use the picnic tables. Visit the **Second Street Café** (189 7th Ave., tel. 718/369–6928) for lunch or brunch. Order soup and some raisin-studded bread pudding. Try **Two Boots** (514 2nd St., tel. 718/499–3253) for creative pizzas (including Cajun and pizza-face personalized pies), Mac and Cheese Louise, or, for adventurous kids, pasta jambalaya. (Can you guess why it's called Two Boots?) **Tom's Restaurant** (782 Washington Ave., tel. 718/636–9738) is a family business with a friendly waitstaff and hearty diner fare.

PUPPETWORKS

For more than 35 years, the Puppetworks, Inc., under the artistic direction of Nicolas Coppola, has been known throughout the country for its mostly marionette productions. In 1987 Puppetworks opened a permanent 75-seat theater in a Park Slope (Brooklyn) storefront, next to the Puppetworks workshop. This informal and family-friendly theater presents daily performances of children's literature classics, with weekdays reserved for groups (20 or more). Puppetworks also hosts private showings of their programs for on-site birthday parties on weekends from 3:45 to 6:15. You supply the cake; they supply the entertainment and the cleanup.

Classic puppet theater favorites like **Puss in Boots** and **Pinocchio** may round out a year-round season that might also include the **Wizard of Oz**, **The Frog Prince**, **Peter and the Wolf**, and **The Emperor's Nightingale.** Each production is faithful to its source, whether it's children's literature or international or national fairy- or folktales.

MAKE THE MOST OF YOUR TIME The walls of the Brooklyn
Puppetworks theater display close to 100 marionettes used in past performances, though many are reused and recostumed. Can your children identify the characters or the stories they come from? Age recommendations for each performance are listed on the Web site along with a schedule of shows, dates, and times. The performances here are interactive with nothing scary, so no need to worry about nightmares.

338 6th Ave., at 4th St., Brooklyn

 $8 adults, $7 children 17 and under

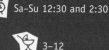 Sa–Su 12:30 and 2:30

718/965–3391; www.puppetworks.org

3–12

Just two puppeteers are responsible for each performance, and while each show averages 13 puppet characters, some have had up to 68 puppets. Professionally designed sets with distinctive painted backdrops and intricate puppet costumes give the feeling of a slightly scaled-down Broadway show. At the end of many performances, a professional puppeteer will bring out one of the beautiful, hand-carved puppets to show to the audience, giving a brief behind-the-scenes—or, more accurately, above-the-strings—talk about the workings of a puppet theater. Children are encouraged to ask questions. If your kids are truly enchanted by the experience, you can purchase a whimsical hand or string puppet on the Web site. Though not made by Puppetworks, these puppets are quite appealing—budget-wise too. Prices range from $3 to $20.

If you like this site, you may also like the New Victory Theater (#29).

EATS FOR KIDS

For comfort food and diner delights (fluffy Belgian waffles, bacon-wrapped meat loaf, and stick-to-your ribs BBQ ribs), visit **Dizzy's** (511 9th St., tel. 718/499–1966). **Tomato and Basil** (226 4th Ave., tel. 718/596–8855) is ripe for pizza and **Miriam** (79 5th Ave., tel. 718/622–2250) is delicious for Israeli cuisine or breakfast eggs and omelets anytime.

KEEP IN MIND Since 1976, when Macy's built a gingerbread puppet theater for Puppetworks, more than 50,000 children and their families have attended the annual Puppetworks Christmas performances. Bring your family to the ninth floor of Macy's Herald Square (Broadway at 34th St., tel. 212/695–4400) and start a new tradition. The holiday-theme performances are given 10 times daily and cost only a few dollars. In 1999 Macy's built a new puppet theater for these always festive and well-attended family puppet programs.

QUEENS COUNTY FARM MUSEUM

A farm in New York City? Just barely. At the very edge of Queens, the Queens County Farm Museum occupies New York City's largest remaining tract of natural, undisturbed farmland. The landmark farmhouse and the 7-acre farmyard that make up the museum are just a small piece of the 47-acre Adriance Farm Park. Here your children can see New York City's only working Steel Windmill and learn how wells and this type of windmill work. You'll also see seasonal field crops (corn, pumpkins, tomatoes), farm tractors and tools, and most fun of all—farm livestock—all without leaving the City.

The farm was started in 1772 and passed through a series of owners until 1927, when New York State purchased the farm for Creedmoor Psychiatric Hospital, to provide both fresh produce and therapy for its patients. Staff and patients raised crops and livestock until the program was discontinued in 1960. Through the Colonial Farmhouse Restoration Society of Bellerose, organized in 1975, the farm's historic structures were preserved and the site was turned into a city park.

KEEP IN MIND Contribute to the Fund-A-Friend program, and your children will get take-away certificates and have their names displayed at the farm. Funds raised are used for feed and veterinary care, from $12 for a chicken or duck to $100 annually for a "caretaker," which helps all the animals.

MAKE THE MOST OF YOUR TIME Check the museum's Web site or call before your visit to see if hayrides, special exhibits, demonstrations like sheep shearing or other activities are scheduled. Some programs carry fees and require reservations. To extend your time in the area, consider a visit to the New York Hall of Science (#23), 10 miles from the Farm Museum. Also, the Alley Pond Environmental Center (228–06 Northern Blvd., Douglaston) is 3 miles away and has informative exhibits and marshland tours.

73–50 Little Neck Pkwy.,
Floral Park

 718/347–FARM;
www.queensfarm.org

 Free; some events charge

 M–F 9–5 outdoors only,
Sa–Su 10–5 house tours

 1 and up

Pick up a map and take a self-guided tour of the farm museum. Begin at the centerpiece of the restored farm: the colonial farmhouse, where much of the original 18th-century plank floors, beamed ceilings, wainscoting, paneling, doors, window glass, and hardware has survived. Other areas available for touring include the duck pond, the herb garden, and the orchard. A chicken coop houses 100 free-range hens producing 260–290 large brown eggs each laying cycle. The eggs are collected daily and washed and boxed for sale. Your youngest children will enjoy a visit with Daisy, an Ayreshire cow, in the cow shed. Next, stroll by the sheep pastures to survey the grazing livestock.

Each season the farm wears a new face, whether it's welcoming newborn barn animals in spring or picking the fresh produce of summer, crunching a crispy autumn apple, or stomping through the snow paths in winter. The Queens County Farm Museum offers a thick slice of farm life to you and your family, painting a picture of the city's rich agricultural past.

If you like this site you may like Historic Richmond Town (#43).

EATS FOR KIDS You can't beat the price or the selection at **Crabtree's Restaurant** (226 Jericho Turnpike, Floral Park, tel. 516/326–7769). Or visit **Nick and Maggies** (265–11 Union Turnpike, New Hyde Park, tel. 516/347–4846), a family-friendly steak house 1 mile away. Hop on over to **IHOP** (248–16 Northern Blvd., Little Neck, tel. 718/224–1178), short for the International House of Pancakes, to indulge in breakfast all day long. It's a good bet overall for finicky eaters.

QUEENS ZOO

Once upon a time, Flushing Meadow played host to the 1964 World's Fair. A zoo opened on the fairgrounds in 1968, and in 1992 it was completely revamped, transforming itself into this small but friendly 11-acre zoo, home to 400 animals of some 40 species and run by the Wildlife Conservation Society. Here you can come face-to-face with a mountain lion, see South American spectacled bears at play, and watch Roosevelt elk roaming the range.

Check for postings of shows at the Wildlife Theater, which include songs, audience participation, and educational programs for the animal-lover in you and your children. They're given Memorial Day–Labor Day, Thursday–Monday and lots of fun for all ages. You also won't want to miss sea lion feedings daily at 11:15, 2, and 4. A highlight for parents and grandparents who remember the World's Fair here, but also for your children who've never seen anything like this, don't miss the zoo's walk-through aviary (a geodesic dome designed by Buckminster Fuller for the World's Fair). You'll see a variety of birds.

MAKE THE MOST OF YOUR TIME The zoo is next to the New York Hall of Science (#23), both in Flushing Meadow Corona Park. Combine your visit to either place with a stop at the nearby Queens Museum of Art (New York City Building, tel. 718/592-9700) to see the 9,335-square-foot scale model of New York City—complete with 895,000 tiny buildings and landmarks—originally made for the 1964 World's Fair.

53-51 111th St., Flushing
Meadows–Corona Park,
Flushing, Queens

718/271-1500;
www.queenszoo.com

$6 ages 13 and up,
$2 children 3–12

Early Apr–late Oct, M–F 10–5,
Sa–Su 10–5:30; late Oct–early Apr,
daily 10–4:30

All ages

Other highlights for your young animal explorers include the marsh exhibit habitat for ducks, geese, herons, egrets, and turtles. A waterfall, additional trees, and rock formations highlight the habitat for the endangered South American spectacled bears. And don't forget to say hi to Claire II, the bald eagle named for former Queens Borough President Claire Shulman.

On the domestic side of the zoo, the toddler set and early grades will enjoy getting up close and personal with the goats, sheep, and rabbits in an inviting planted space where they can also see a llama, Vietnamese pot-bellied pig, donkeys, and such feathered friends as a Peking duck and a Rhode Island Red. Despite its size, the zoo offers something for just about everyone.

If you like this sight you may also like the Staten Island Zoo (#5).

KEEP IN MIND Try to visit Otis, the famous coyote rescued in Central Park in 1999. He's taken up residence here at the Queens Zoo.

EATS FOR KIDS Feed your animal appetite at the **cafeteria,** overlooking the sea lion pool. Visit **Gum Fung** (136-28 39th Ave., tel. 718/762–8821) for dim sum or grab a vanilla and hot fudge shake at **Joe's Best Burger** (39–11 Main St., tel. 718/445–8665) or try the **Omonia Café** (32–20 Broadway, Astoria, tel. 718/274–6650) for a light bite and people-watching.

RADIO CITY MUSIC HALL

You may have watched an awards show broadcast from Radio City Music Hall or even attended a performance here, but to get behind the scenes of this lavish art deco palace that's home to the high-kicking, smart-stepping Radio City Rockettes, you'll want to take the Stage Door Tour. The brainchild of theatrical impresario S. L. "Roxy" Rothafel, owner of New York's Roxy Theater, Radio City was the first building in the Rockefeller Center complex and the world's largest indoor theater in 1932. In 1999 it was renovated at a cost of $70 million. Tours showcase the building's technological capabilities as well as its history. Luminaries such as Frank Sinatra, Ella Fitzgerald, and Sammy Davis Jr., have graced this stage, as have contemporary artists including Bette Midler, Sting, and 98 Degrees.

To whet your appetite, here are some amazing Radio City facts: Some of the curtains can create steam and rain, and the shimmering gold curtain is the largest theatrical curtain on earth. The mighty Wurlitzer organ, built in 1932, has two consoles, each weighing 2½ tons. Its pipes, some of which are 32 feet tall, are housed in 11 rooms. Look up

MAKE THE MOST OF YOUR TIME

Visiting Radio City Music Hall during the winter months is magical. Window shop at the holiday decorated department stores on Fifth Avenue, stop for hot chestnuts or a pretzel, or browse at FAO Schwarz (#47).

EATS FOR KIDS Take your pick (or your children's pick) of local theme restaurants, each with eye-appealing memorabilia and kid fare. Music fans sing the praises of the **Hard Rock Cafe** (1501 Broadway., tel. 212/343–3355). Movie buffs marvel at **Planet Hollywood** (1540 Broadway, tel. 212/333–7827). Board a spaceship to planet Mars for a crater burger, galactic cheese sandwich, or full moon pizza at **Mars 2112** (1633 Broadway, tel. 212/582–2112).

1260 6th Ave., at 50th St.

 212/247-4777 tour, 212/307-7171 events; www.radiocity.com

 Tour $17 ages 12 and up, $10 children 11 and under

 Tours daily 11–3 every ½ hr

 7 and up

and you can see a 24-carat gold-leaf ceiling glistening 60 feet above you. For the electrical record, the music hall contains over 25,000 lightbulbs inside; outside, the marquee is a block long and has more than 6 miles of red and blue neon.

The Stage Door Tour also includes a visit to the private apartment of founder Roxy Rothafel and a stop in the costume shop, which contains examples of lustrous outfits worn by the Rockettes, the world's most famous precision dance troupe and stars of America's most beloved holiday show the *Radio City Christmas Spectacular*. Your tour group will also meet a member of the Radio City Rockettes, who will share some of the company's history. One-hour tours depart from the main lobby at the corner of 6th Avenue and 50th Street.

If you like this sight you may also enjoy Kupferberg Center Performances (#40).

KEEP IN MIND In 1979, to save the music hall from the wrecking ball, the program format was changed from films and stage shows to live concerts, television specials, and events. The Radio City Christmas Spectacular, Blues Clues, Dora the Explorer, and adult as well as kid concerts play to sell-out crowds throughout the year. You must purchase a ticket for children 2 and older for performances here, but for some events, like Barney, youngsters 1 and older require a ticket, even if they plan to sit in your lap for most of the show.

ROCKEFELLER CENTER AND THE ICE RINK

Skating at the Ice Rink at Rockefeller Plaza is enchanting, twinkling, festive, and fun, and it's spectacular when the huge Christmas tree casts its long shadow. (It arrives in mid-November, and the lighting ceremony is shortly after Thanksgiving.) It may not be the biggest rink in the world, but skating here certainly is one of the big New York experiences. Sessions are 1½ hours, and admission is on a first-come, first-served basis. Skate and locker rentals, season passes and multiticket books, lessons, and group rates are all available, as are birthday parties with skate admissions, rental, and refreshments (January–April). Teens get a bit exuberant during evening skates and the pace is faster.

If you're planning to be at the rink for an early-morning skate, NBC's *Today Show* broadcasts from a ground-floor glass-enclosed studio at 49th Street and Rockefeller Plaza. Be here between 7 and 9 AM to try to join the backdrop of faces behind the show's hosts. Bring a colorful sign championing your hometown and you might end up on TV.

MAKE THE MOST OF YOUR TIME Monday through Thursday, lunchtime skating is a bargain at $5. Not quite a bargain, but worth a peek if you haven't gone to the top of the Empire State Building (#48), is the Top of the Rock (30 Rockefeller Plaza, tel. 212/698–2000); its 6 level observatory has floor-to-ceiling windows permitting breathtaking views of city landmarks. Tickets are $17.50 for adults and $11.25 for children 6–12.

Bordered by 47th and 52nd Sts. and 5th and 7th Aves.; ice rink, between 49th and 50th Sts. and 5th and 6th Aves.

212/332-7654 rink, 212/332-7655 lessons, 212/664-7174 tours

 Skating $10–$14 ages 12 and up, $7.50–$8.50 children 11 and under; skate rental $7.50

M–F 9 AM–12 AM, Sa–Su 8:30 AM–12 AM; call for session times

 2 and up

But the ice rink is just a small part of the 22-acre complex known as Rockefeller Center, one of the world's most famous pieces of real estate. There are actually 19 limestone and aluminum buildings here, and tours of the complex as well as combination tickets including a tour of NBC Studios are available. Or explore the center on your own, before or after your skating session.

This complex is also home to three famous statues from Greek mythology. Atlas stands guard outside the International Building (5th Ave. between 50th and 51st Sts.). On the Lower Plaza is the famous gold-leaf statue of Prometheus. The entrance of the 70-story GE Building (aka "30 Rock") is also guarded by another striking statue of Prometheus. It all makes Rockefeller Center a landmark of epic proportions.

If you like this site you may also like the NBC Studios Tour (#30).

EATS FOR KIDS
Dine at the **Rink Cafe and Bar**, open in summer 11–11, or the **Rock Center Café** (tel. 212/332–7620) year-round. **Dean & DeLuca** (1 Rockefeller Plaza, tel. 212/664–1363) serves quick sandwiches and snacks.

KEEP IN MIND Other great spots for a twirl on the ice are the Lasker and Wollman Memorial rinks (see Central Park, #57); Sky Rink (see Chelsea Piers (#55), tel. 212/336–6100); the World's Fair Ice Skating Rink (New York City Building, south wing, Flushing Meadows–Corona Park, Queens, tel. 718/271–1996); the Staten Island Skating Pavilion (30–80 Arthur Kill Rd., Staten Island, tel. 718/948–4800) for year-round fun; and Brooklyn's Wollman Rink (see Prospect Park, #17), not to be confused with the Wollman Memorial Rink in Central Park. Contact each for prices, hours, and seasons.

RYE PLAYLAND

Go for the rides. Go for the fun. Go to sun, swim, play, or walk around, but go to Rye Playland.

This National Historic Landmark, maintained by the Westchester County Parks Department, has the distinction of being the only government-owned amusement park. It opened in 1928 and has since permeated popular culture by popping up in such films as *Big*, *Fatal Attraction*, and *Sweet and Lowdown*. Remarkably, the park still maintains seven of its original rides among its current 50; newbies over the years have included vertical thrill rides, water rides, and a separate Kiddyland just for the toddler set.

The carousel, built in 1915, is still going strong, and the trademark 82-foot Dragon Coaster is one of the last remaining historic wooden coasters in North America. Two can't-misses for the not-easily-queasy are the SuperFlight Flying Coaster (minimum height 50") and Catch-a-Wave (minimum height 48", 42" with adult), a high-speed rotating platform

EATS FOR KIDS

It's hard to imagine coming here without letting your children sip slushies or get sticky with cotton candy for a snack break. There are sit-down tables and fast food galore throughout Playland, including favorites from fast-food giants. You can also pack a lunch.

MAKE THE MOST OF YOUR TIME

Remember to bring all the essentials: swimsuits, towels, beach toys, sunscreen, and water bottles—especially for your younger thrill seekers. Unlike the rest of this beautifully landscaped park, Kiddyland has no natural shade (or cool breezes). Bring blankets or lawn or beach chairs if you're staying for a concert. And of course, bring money. Parking costs $5 weekdays, $7 weekends, and to ride the rides you can purchase 8-hour Fun Bands ($40) or Fun Cards with 24 points ($20) or 38 points ($30) with different points for each ride. Look for discount coupons in local magazines and newspapers.

Playland Pkwy., Rye Beach

 Free; most attractions charge

 914/813-7000;
www.ryeplayland.org

 May–Sept, T–Su, hrs vary seasonally

 All ages

thrill ride. Also at the park are arcade games, the usual midway games, a lake with boat rides, minigolf, a beach, a scenic boardwalk, and an Olympic-size pool, all on Long Island Sound.

Rides usually open at noon, and Tuesday through Friday (the park is closed Monday, except for summer holidays and special events) is less crowded than weekends. Watch for costumed characters and strolling musicians, and catch a puppet show at the Kiddyland Puppet Theater. Be warned that Kiddyland gets crowded by midday, so you'll want to visit early or at dinnertime. Fireworks displays are held every Wednesday and Friday night in July and August. For the best viewing check out the Boardwalk by the Log Flume and the Playland Plunge.

If you like this site you may also like Coney Island (#51).

KEEP IN MIND Recent accidents at Playland remind parents to put safety first when visiting an amusement park. Adhere to the height requirements for each ride. Accompany your young children on rides and use good judgment if allowing them to ride with a friend or sibling. Be sure seat belts and safety harnesses are properly buckled. Be sure you and your child watch a ride before jumping on. Determine if your child will be scared or uncomfortable and when in doubt, stay off the rides that cause you or your children concern.

SCHOMBURG CENTER

The Schomburg Center for Research in Black Culture, one of the research libraries of the New York Public Library system, is considered one of the leading institutions of its kind in the world. Devoted to the preservation of materials on black life, it's the guardian of more than five million items, including more than 3.5 million manuscript items, 170,000 books, and 750,000 photographs. Collections of magazines, posters, art objects, films, videotapes, audio recordings, and memorabilia are also included.

Tours, exhibitions, forums, film screenings, and performing arts bring black history and culture to life for both young and old. The Schomburg Center sponsors more than 60 public programs each year, including staged readings, plays, book celebrations, concerts, lectures, and panel discussions, many of which will appeal to middle schoolers and high schoolers. Regular exhibitions are mounted in the Latimer/Edison Gallery or the Exhibition Hall. The Art and Artifacts collection holds more than 20,000 items in three areas: paintings and sculpture, works on paper, and textiles and artifacts. It's particularly strong in art produced

MAKE THE MOST OF YOUR TIME Other Harlem sights include the Abyssinian Baptist Church (132 Odell Clark Pl. W, tel. 212/862–7474), pulpit for two famous Adam Clayton Powells, one of whom was also a congressman. Tour the Apollo Theatre (253 W. 125th St., tel. 212/531–5337). The Studio Museum in Harlem (144 W. 125th St., tel. 212/864–4500), a small art museum, has a sculpture garden and a collection of paintings and photographs.

 515 Malcolm X Blvd.

212/491-2200;
www.schomburgcenter.org

 Free

 M–W 12–8, Th–F 11–6, Sa 10–5

 9 and up

during the Harlem Renaissance. Portraits of many famous 19th- and 20th-century black artists, politicians, actors, musicians, athletes, and social activists are included.

People of African descent are celebrated here in exhibitions, special events, manuscripts, archives, moving images and recorded sound. Can't get here to visit? Many past exhibitions like Malcolm X: A Search for Truth and In Motion: The African-American Migration Experience are featured in the Schomburg's online exhibitions (www.schomburgcenter.org). If your knowledge is lacking, there's no better place to learn about the influence of black Americans on our history and culture than the Schomburg Center.

If you like this site you may also like the Studio Museum in Harlem (144 West 125th Street, 212/864-4500, www.studiomuseum.org).

EATS FOR KIDS
Go to **Manna's Deli Restaurant** (486 Lenox Ave., tel. 212/234-4488) for breakfast, salad bar, fried chicken, and soul food buffets. For southern specialties, home-style cooking, and friendly service, try **Miss Maude's Spoonbread Two** (547 Lenox Ave., tel. 212/690-3100) or world-famous **Sylvia's** (328 Lenox Ave., tel. 212/996-0660).

KEEP IN MIND The Junior Scholars Program (tel. 212/491-2294) meets on Saturday for 26 weeks 10-3. It's an intensive and ambitious series geared to students of African descent and its goal is to ground young people in the histories and cultures of people in the African Diaspora. Workshops in music, theater, dance, video, publishing, photography, visual arts, and Web design are offered.

SONY WONDER TECHNOLOGY LAB

From the moment you're accosted in the lobby atrium of Sony Wonder Technology Lab by greeter b.b. wonderbot, the interactive robot, you feel the excitement of cutting-edge communication technology. After picking up a free timed ticket from a desk by the elevator, you might have to wait a few minutes before an attendant escorts you to the fourth floor log-in stations, where you'll enter your name, have your picture taken, and record your voice; all of this information will be encoded on your personalized, souvenir swipe card, which enables you to access the interactive exhibits. There might be a bit of line at log-in, too: your kids can amuse themselves by ogling all the fiber-optic lights encased in the walls.

For a historical perspective, the Communications Bridge, aka the fourth-floor walkway, covers 150 years in the history and development of technology.

KEEP IN MIND July and August are the busiest times here, but you can guarantee your admission and save time by reserving admission one week to one month ahead by calling 212/833–5414. Also: exits are final. Once you leave you cannot come back in unless you join the (possibly long) line again to reenter.

MAKE THE MOST OF YOUR TIME Progression through the museum logically follows from the fourth floor; the exhibits are arranged throughout several levels over the next two floors, accessible by walkway ramps, so you won't have to board the elevator again (though there's also an elevator on floor 3) until you log out on the second floor. As you walk through, the recurring fun will come largely from your swipe cards: you and your kids will see your pictures or hear your voices pop up as you swipe.

 550 Madison Ave.

 Free

212/833-8100;
www.sonywondertechlab.com

Sa 10–5, Su 12–

All age

On the third floor's upper level your 7- to 17-year-olds can take part in a production in the television studio, video editing and creating their own movie trailers using real film clips from Sony Pictures. If the 72-seat High Definition Theater (at the foot of the third-floor ramp's lower level) is in between showings, check out the challenging computer simulations at the Environmental Command Center.

If you can manage to bypass the hordes at Playstation stations on the second floor, the sweet high point of this level is the Wonder of Music, where you and your kids can enter a glass studio, choose from a keyboard, bass, sax, or drum, rehearse, and then perform for an excited audience.

If you like this site you may also like the Museum of the Moving Image (#32).

EATS FOR KIDS In Sony Plaza, **Starbucks** offers sandwiches and pastries. **Illy's** offers similar items that are kosher. **City Market Café** (551 Madison Ave., tel.212/572–9800) has a create-your-own salad bar, homemade pizza and much, much more. (Other locations at 178 5th Ave., 48 W. 48th St., and 1100 Madison Ave.) If you can brave the often long lines, visit **Serendipity 3** (225 E. 60th St., tel. 212/838–3531) for dessert and ice-cream treats.

Nestled within a 12-block historic district of restored 18th- and 19th-century buildings and sailing ships, this museum actually comprises a number of facilities in a historic district much like a large pedestrian mall with a myriad of places and spaces to explore. Stop first at the visitor center to get your bearings, maps, tickets, tour routes, and exhibit information and lace up your walking shoes.

Young and old may first wish to set sail for another place and time aboard two historic stationary museum vessels open for tours, the *Peking* (a large sailing cargo ship) and a lightship, the *Ambrose*. You can explore the harbor on the *W.O. Decker*, a 1930 tugboat that worked this waterfront. Or climb aboard the *Pioneer*, a historic schooner, for a fun-filled sail. Sailing instruction for teens is offered on the *Lettie G. Howard*, a fully restored 1893 fishing schooner, now a National Historic Landmark.

MAKE THE MOST OF YOUR TIME If a visit here tickled your sails, why not come back for more? Learn to furl a sail, tie a knot, or chart a course at one of the family programs scheduled every Saturday and Sunday throughout the year. Programs are geared to children 4 and up and are free with museum admission. Recent series have included maritime crafts in Art of the High Seas and exploration, experimentation and investigation in the Seaport Family Science Series. From the South Street Seaport it's just a hop, skip, and a jump to many other local attractions.

Pier 16 Visitors' Center,
12 Fulton St.

 $8 ages 13 and up,
children 5–12 $4,
under 5 free

 Daily 10–5

212/748-8600;
www.southstseaportmuseum.org

3 and up

Your family can visit the Maritime Crafts Center, where model-builders and a wood-carver ply their trades. At Bowne & Company Stationers (2112 Water St.), a re-creation of a 19th-century printing shop, artisans demonstrate the skills that made the city the nation's printing capital. On weekends, holidays, and school vacations, crafts workshops related to museum themes and exhibits are held. Performers and storytellers are also featured. Three floors of galleries in the landmark Schermerhorn Row, a redbrick terrace of Georgian and Federal warehouses and counting houses, feature artifacts, fine, and decorative folk arts, ship models, scrimshaw, and maps, as well as restaurants and shops. Teens will enjoy it here but also want to head to the shops and eateries of Pier 17. Street performances, concerts, and special events all take place against a backdrop of history chronicling New York's original seaport and its commercial and cultural impact on the city.

If you like this site you might also like the Fraunces Tavern Museum (#44).

KEEP IN MIND For an interesting look below the surface, visit NY Unearthed (17 State St., tel. 212/748-8757). This urban archaeology center lets you ride a glass-enclosed elevator in a conservation lab offering a 3-D cross section of an archaeology site. Individual visits are only allowed during regularly scheduled public programs, so call ahead.

EATS FOR KIDS The Seaport is home to more than 35 restaurants and eateries from fast food to restaurant fare. Grab a burger, hot dog, pizza, or salad at the **Promenade Food Court** (Pier 17, 3rd fl.). Don't miss the view from the tables in the glass-walled atrium. If deep dish is your wish, try **Pizzeria Uno Chicago** (89 South St., Pier 17, tel. 212/791-7999). Encourage your children to use the bathrooms at restaurants here. They tend to be tidier than the public restrooms.

STATEN ISLAND CHILDREN'S MUSEUM

How would your children like to crawl through an ant home, watch a butterfly being born, or listen to an insect chorus? They can do that and more at the Staten Island Children's Museum. In an 82-acre park, the museum occupies 40,000 square feet of a four-story building with an Italianate facade and a renovated barn and connector building. An imposing porpoise, hanging in the central atrium, greets you. Exhibits tackle subjects from many different perspectives, incorporating the arts, science, and the humanities with an inviting child-friendly approach.

The Bugs and Other Insects exhibit invites big and not-so-big people into the miniature world of insects. If insects bug your kids, a quick trip to Block Harbor will put them back on an even keel. This waterfront setting, complete with pirate ship and gangplank, is an imaginative play space containing blocks and a menagerie of animal toys. In It's a Dog's Life, kids learn about animals' amazing abilities and body language as they see like a pigeon, hear like a cat, and smell like a dog. Daily storytelling and animal feedings are held here.

EATS FOR KIDS Visit the **Snack Zone** café here, open 1–2 Tuesday through Friday. **Ozon**, a healthy-fare fast-food restaurant in the lower plaza here, serves fun food in a cool place. You can get killer chili at **Adobe Blues Restaurant** (63 Lafayette St., tel. 718/720–2583), a southwestern-style eating place just off Richmond Terrace.

MAKE THE MOST OF YOUR TIME The museum is in the Snug Harbor Cultural Center in the midst of a National Historic Landmark park. In planning your visit here you can also visit the Newhouse Center for Contemporary Art (tel. 718/448–2500), the beaux arts–style music hall for a variety of performances in drama and music (tel. 718/815–SNUG), the Art Lab School (tel. 718/447–8667) for classes or the Staten Island Botanical Garden (tel. 718/273–8200). For tours, visitor information, or special event details you can also call the Snug Harbor Cultural Center (718/448–2500).

Snug Harbor Cultural Center,
1000 Richmond Terr., Staten Island

 $5 ages 1 and up

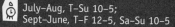 July–Aug, T–Su 10–5;
Sept–June, T–F 12–5, Sa–Su 10–5

 718/273–2060;
www.statenislandkids.org

 1 and up

Kids can jump on a fire truck, ring its bell, and slide down a firehouse pole in the Ladder 11 exhibit. Kids 5 and up will particularly enjoy Portia's Playhouse, an interactive theater space where kids try on masks or costumes and use props, puppets, sound effects, lights, and other theater equipment in imaginative play. The Walk-In! Workshop is a classroom activity center equipped with self-directed art activities and materials. In Great Explorations, three environments—tundra, rain forest, and ocean—let little tykes go on adventures, from driving a dogsled to diving deep to the ocean floor. Sea of Boats, an outdoor play space, includes a tugboat, lighthouse, dinghy, and other nautical knickknacks, weather permitting.

Museum educators are always on hand to animate and explain exhibit themes and activities. Family workshops, hands-on science activities, and performances are also part of the fun and learning here.

If you like this site you might also like the Children's Museum of Manhattan (#54).

KEEP IN MIND There are so many different ways to "do" this museum. Want to watch the stars come out here? The museum sponsors sleep-overs. Feel like celebrating? You can have a birthday party here, perhaps based on a museum exhibit, or a cooking, a chocolate, or an ice-cream party, too. Benefits of a family membership ($80) include advance notice of special events, sneak previews of new exhibits, members-only events, the museum calendar, and discounts on gift shop items, birthday parties, special programs, and summer minicamps.

STATEN ISLAND ZOO

5

How many legs does an African millipede have? How far can a snowy owl turn its head? For the answers to these and other animal queries, visit the Staten Island Zoo. On 8 acres in a manicured park setting, New York City's biggest little zoo features an African savanna, aquarium, and tropical forest. If you love things that slink and slither, check out the Carl Kaufeld Serpentarium, with an internationally acclaimed display of reptiles. In fact, it has one of the most extensive collections of North American rattlesnakes anywhere and it's a must-see here at the zoo. Come on Wednesday afternoons and it's free—even better!

The African Savannah exhibit re-creates this ecosystem at twilight and features meerkats, a burrowing python, leopards, bush babies, and rock hyrax—curious creatures that look like rodents but are actually most closely related to elephants. The meerkat habitat is getting a makeover with glass walls that will facilitate viewing. Children 2 to 10 will be mesmerized with the meerkat digging and pop-ups, reminding them of the arcade game "Whack a Mole." The Tropical Forest exhibit highlights the endangered South American rain forest and the

EATS FOR KIDS Visit the **Zoo Café** (tel. 718/720–7218) for a convenient lunch or midday snack. Try **Duffy's** (650 Forest Ave., tel. 718/447–9276) for Staten Island's best burger and family dining. No reservations are taken, so expect a wait. **Nucci's Italian Restaurant** (616 Forest Ave., tel. 781/815–4882) is the place for pizza and Italian fare.

animals that dwell within. Here your family can watch the piranha, spider monkeys, short-tailed leaf-nosed fruit bats, and iguanas in a natural flow of flora and fauna. A must-see is the Otter Exhibit, where North American River Otters perform their antics from above and below the underwater viewing tank.

The wraparound aquarium exhibit spotlights marine life from all over the world; the Children's Center, a favorite of the toddler set, resembles a New England farm, complete with a covered bridge overlooking a duck pond. Here your children can meet an interesting array of international domestic farm animals. Be sure to visit the Pony Barn and Track for pony rides (additional fee).

If you like this sight, you may also like the Central Park Zoo (#56).

MAKE THE MOST OF YOUR TIME

Plan your day at the zoo so you don't miss the action during feeding times. To see when the reptiles chow down, when the sharks and piranhas break for a bite, or when the bats need a nibble, check the feeding time schedules listed at the entry gates.

KEEP IN MIND If your child, like my elephant sanctuary supporter and strict vegetarian, is an animal activist, you can become a monkey's uncle here at the zoo. You can adopt a zoo resident for a $35 to $100 fee, which pays for the care and feeding of your favorite friend. Your child will get a photo, fact sheet, profile of your animal and adoption certificate. No, they don't get to go home on family visits.

STATUE OF LIBERTY

4

For more than 100 years this historic monument, one of our nation's most heavily visited attractions, has served as a universal beacon of hope and opportunity, a symbol of freedom, and a gift of international friendship. Sculpted by Frederic-Auguste Bartholdi, and built in 1884 in France, the statue stood in Paris until it was dismantled and sent to the United States in 1885. A foundation and pedestal were created here, and the completed monument was dedicated on October 28, 1886.

Kids 8 and up may enjoy a ranger-guided tour. The promenade tour includes the museum in the pedestal's lobby, where the statue's original torch resides, as well as a visit to the promenade, which has great views of the statue and New York Harbor. The observatory tour covers much of the promenade tour plus an elevator ride to the pedestal observatory, with more awesome views, and a lighted view up into the copper interior of the statue. Kids 7–12 who may be impatient in a lengthy group presentation may be happier taking their own self-guided tour as a Junior Ranger; a free booklet, available at the Liberty Island Information Center walks kids through the tour.

MAKE THE MOST OF YOUR TIME

In summer, waiting in line can be hard on kids; bring water bottles, juice boxes, and small toys to amuse them. Saturday is more crowded than Sunday. The ticket office for both the Statue of Liberty and Ellis Island ferry service is at Castle Clinton National Monument (see #58).

EATS FOR KIDS There's a pleasant outdoor **café** on Liberty Island. You can also pack a picnic to eat along the way, or after your return on the ferry, go to **Alphanoose** (8 Maiden Lane, tel. 212/528–4669) for Middle Eastern cuisine, including falafels, pitas, hummus and sumptuous soup.

Liberty Island, New York Harbor

Tickets and monument passes
 (877-LADY TIX, www.statuecruises.com);
Statue of Liberty information
(212/363–3200, www.nps.gov)

 Free; ferry fees $11.50 ages
13 and up, $4.50 children 4–12;
time passes required to enter
the Statue of Liberty but not
required to visit Ellis Island.

Daily 9–5

 4 and up

One of the main reasons to visit the statue, of course, is to view this monument to freedom up close. A museum here features exhibits detailing how the statue was built, and the promenade, colonnade, and top level of the pedestal offer spectacular views of New York Harbor. Life-size castings of the face and foot of the statue are available for sight-impaired visitors to feel. A "time pass" reservation system is run by the National Park Service for visitors who want to enter the monument. Time passes are not required to visit the grounds. A limited number of time passes are available from the ferry company daily on a first-come, first-served basis. Or you can get a time-pass reservation online by visiting www.statuereservations.com. As she always has, Lady Liberty welcomes all.

If you like this site you may also like Ellis Island (#49).

KEEP IN MIND No large backpacks are allowed on the ferry. What is a large backpack? Any pack that can't fit into a standard plastic milk crate. No strollers or backpacks are allowed in the monument either. Lockers for small items are available on Liberty Island, but don't forget to retrieve your belongings before leaving for home.

THEODORE ROOSEVELT BIRTHPLACE

Though the building here isn't the real brownstone where Teddy Roosevelt was born—it's a 1923 reconstruction—it does teach a lot about the real life of the nation's 26th president. Five period rooms—the library, dining room, parlor (the most elegant room in the house), master bedroom, and nursery—are furnished with many items from the original house, pieces belonging to other family members, and other decorative period pieces. The nursery will most interest your youngest visitors. Two obelisks in the library are souvenirs of a family trip to Egypt. (Guided tours are given hourly.) In addition, two museum galleries display a variety of historical items, including journals, family photographs, articles of clothing including Roosevelt's Rough Rider uniform, and his crib.

The site offers a window on what mid-19th-century life was like for a wealthy family living on a once-quiet, tree-lined street in a most fashionable New York City neighborhood. Memorabilia reveals much about the man who would become not only president of the United States but also vice president, governor of New York, assistant secretary of the Navy, police

EATS FOR KIDS For a spot of tea, some scones, and a light snack, visit **T Salon & Emporium** (11 E. 20th St., tel. 212/358–0506). For an endless menu, substantial portions, and reasonable prices, try **America** (9 E. 18th St., tel. 212/505–2110). Kids get crayons and coloring books, and a magician and balloon artist perform on weekends. Order a frothy root beer float or the Coca Cola cake and all the comfort foods of home at **Chat n' Chew** (10 E. 16th St., tel. 212/243–1616).

28 E. 20th St.

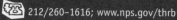 212/260-1616; www.nps.gov/thrb

 $3 ages 17 and up

 T-Sa 9-5

7 and up

commissioner, New York State assemblyman, and Rough Rider, as well as a rancher and cowboy.

As a young child, Theodore, called Teedie by his family, was a thin and sickly child who suffered from severe asthma. His father made the bedroom behind his nursery into an open-air porch by taking out a wall and putting up a railing. He also installed gym equipment so Teedie could exercise and improve his health. Roosevelt and friends used to climb through the nursery windows to get to the outdoor porch and equipment. He obviously overcame his frailty.

If you like this sight you may also like Federal Hall National Memorial (#46).

MAKE THE MOST OF YOUR TIME

Those interested in following TR through his later years should visit the Sagamore Hill National Historic Site (Cove Neck Rd., Oyster Bay, tel. 516/922-4788), on Long Island. Roosevelt's home for most of his adult life, it contains original furnishings and memorabilia.

KEEP IN MIND The historic objects in this museum, as in most, are quite fragile and should not be touched. This is sometimes a difficult impulse for children to master and sometimes equally difficult for adults. A close friend fatefully relates the museum tale of touching the frame of a picture on display, which immediately set off earsplitting alarms and caused gates to come crashing down, barring the exits to the museum. If some among your brood have selective hearing, this "don't touch" story might stick with them.

UNITED NATIONS

If you come on a working day, you can see all 191 U.N. members' flags flying above 1st Avenue—from Afghanistan to Zimbabwe. It's an impressive sight, but so is the rest of the United Nations Headquarters. Created in 1945, the U.N. continues to be an international forum where issues such as world peace and the fight against poverty and injustice are discussed.

As you enter headquarters gates, you're leaving the United States and stepping into an "international territory," belonging to all members of the U.N. It has its own fire and security forces and its own postal administration, where you can post only mail bearing U.N. stamps. Children here enjoy mailing a postcard home to themselves as a souvenir.

EATS FOR KIDS The **coffee shop** (public concourse) is open daily. The **Comfort Diner** (214 E. 45th St., tel. 212/867–4555) serves big portions of home-style food.

One-hour guided tours include an explanation of the structure and activities of the organization as well as descriptions of art on the tour route. Tours are given in many languages including the six official languages of the U.N.: Arabic, Chinese, English,

KEEP IN MIND It may be hard to impress upon children the difficulty of people from many places speaking different languages working together toward a common goal of peace. You can illustrate the concept by inviting your children and their friends at home to play with building blocks on the floor silently to see if they can build something. Then have them build, each speaking their "own language" or, for the sake of the exercise, nonsense words, to simulate a variety of people from different places. Finally, ask them to work together all speaking English to get the job done. What insights can they share about this experience?

1st Ave. and 46th St.

 Tour $13.50 ages 15 and up, $7.50 children 5–14

 Daily 9:15–4:45; tour daily, except Jan–Feb, no Sa–Su tour

212/963–TOUR, 212/963–7539 non-English tours; www.un.org

 8 and up, tour 5 and up

French, Russian, and Spanish. See if you can get your kids to memorize that list; it'll be an impressive fact to recite to a teacher one day, and it's bound to come up from time to time.

Tour highlights for children 8 and up include: the General Assembly, where all nations are represented and have assigned seats, and the Security Council Chamber, where the 15 members make decisions on political issues such as peacekeeping missions around the world. These are the two most photographed spots. The tour may also include the Trustee Council Chamber, Economic and Social Council Chamber, Rose Garden, lobby, and public concourse. In the lobby, draw your kids' attention to the gifts that have been given to the U.N. over the years, including a model of Sputnik I from the Soviet Union, a moon rock from the United States, and a 15-foot-by-30-foot stained-glass Chagall window presented by the artist in memory of Secretary General Dag Hammarskjold.

If you like this sight you may also like Ellis Island (#49).

MAKE THE MOST OF YOUR TIME At the U.N.
home page, your school-age children can take an online tour before your visit; get up-to-date information about U.N. work in areas like peace and security, economic and social development, and human rights; and browse press releases and daily highlights, often before printed versions are released. You can also get free publications (in several languages) from the U.N. and many of its agencies and programs.

YANKEE STADIUM

I t's the House that Ruth Built—Babe Ruth, that is—as well as the Home of the Champions. (As of this writing the Yankees hold 26 world titles.) Since April 18, 1923, when the team played its first game here—against the Boston Red Sox—the Yankees have captivated this town in a way few institutions have.

Take them out to the ball game, but come a little early. The park opens up 1½–2 hours before each game, and kids can often score an autograph from a player before the end of batting practice, if they move close to the field. Before the game tour Monument Park, which contains plaques and memorials to the all-time greats: Mickey Mantle, Joe DiMaggio, Lou Gehrig, and the Babe, as well as a tribute plaque remembering September 11.

Even when there's no game, the allure of a tour at Yankee Stadium will delight any baseball aficionado, young or old. The Classic Tour is a one-hour Yankees history lesson with a visit to the dugout, the press box, and Monument Park. When there's no game, you can park free at parking lot 14, the players' lot, across from the press gate.

EATS FOR KIDS Typical ballpark fare is sold for sky-high prices, but part of the fun is partaking. So compromise: bring clear bags (so security can view) of food from home and then parcel out the stadium junk food. For the best ballpark value, look no further than the song: buy some peanuts and Cracker Jack.

MAKE THE MOST OF YOUR TIME Children under 30 inches tall who can walk under a turnstile or can be carried in can attend games free as long as they sit in your lap, but you'll be more comfortable if you spring for seats. Bleacher seats are a mere $10, but are unshaded and, as the name implies, are actual bleachers without seatbacks, and that can get very old very fast; for seven bucks more you can trade up to the Tier Reserved seats; sections 13 and 14 of Tier Reserved are designated alcohol-free family seating. And although this may seem obvious, it's very common: If your kids are 8 and under, remind them to actually watch the game.

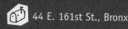 44 E. 161st St., Bronx

 Games $10 and up; tours $15–$25 ages 15 and up, $8–$15 children 14 and under

 Tours M–Sa 10:30–5 except when team plays at home

718/293–4300, 718/298–6000 tours; www.newyorkyankees.com

 5 and up

If you actually want to take in a game—highly recommended—it certainly helps to buy tickets in advance, but don't underestimate how accessible a Yankee game can be at the last minute. You can often show up at game time or a few innings in and get tickets, especially for the beloved bleacher seats (on game day, $12 apiece) or the Tier Reserved sections ($20 apiece on game day).

On August 16, 2006, a groundbreaking ceremony for a new Yankee Stadium was held just across the street from the existing stadium. Slated for completion by Opening Day 2009, the new stadium will be a half-million square feet larger than the existing site with seating for an estimated 50,300 fans.

If you like this site you may also like seeing a sporting event at Madison Square Garden (#36).

KEEP IN MIND Fans do bring their sometimes very young babies to the game (it's that hard to stay away); there are baby-changing facilities in women's and some men's bathrooms on the Field, Main, Loge, and Tier levels. The crowds in the stadium interior can be intense, so guest services provides wristbands to help children identify their seat locations; look for the Tag-A-Kid guest services booths throughout the stadium to get a wristband. Also, check the Yankees Web site to take note of games where promotions or giveaways (caps, stuffed toys, trading cards) are scheduled.

MANY THANKS

I n the '70s, my boyfriend—now husband—and I would joke that we were off on another "family adventure" as we explored parks, museums, and other attractions. No family, of course. Fast-forward many years later and we still take those family adventures, but now with three children in tow. As a parent, a teacher, and writer, I look for those "teachable moments" to share with my children. The first edition of this book was written with a 5-year-old, a 12-year-old, and a 14-year-old by my side with the challenge of finding something of interest for everyone, parents included. Today, the ages have changed, but the challenges remain the same. Keep savoring those teachable moments, and the fun of experiencing them together as a family!

Many thanks to the public relations professionals at each of our sights who were so helpful in answering questions and checking facts. This book is lovingly dedicated to Rachel ("Are we there yet?"); Jennifer ("Can we listen to the car radio instead of those children's songs?"); and Michael ("When are we leaving?").

—Mindy Bailin

ALL AROUND TOWN

SOMETHING FOR EVERYONE

BEST MUSEUM

American Museum of Natural History
Brooklyn Children's Museum
Metropolitan Museum of Art
Museum of Modern Art
South Street Seaport Museum

WACKIEST

Coney Island
F.A.O. Schwarz
Madame Tussaud's Wax Museum
Sony Wonder Technology Lab
Staten Island Children's Museum

BEST BETS

BEST IN TOWN
Bronx Zoo
Central Park
Ellis Island
New York Botanical Garden
New York Hall of Science

BEST OUTDOORS
Brooklyn Botanic Garden
Central Park
Jones Beach
Prospect Park
Rye Playland

BEST CULTURAL ACTIVITY
Broadway on a Budget
Metropolitan Museum of Art
Museum of Modern Art
New York City Opera Young People's Workshops
Radio City Music Hall

GOOD TIMES GALORE

WIGGLE & GIGGLE Give your kids a chance to stick out their tongues at you. Start by making a face, then have the next person imitate you and add a gesture of his own—snapping fingers, winking, clapping, sneezing, or the like. The next person mimics the first two and adds a third gesture, and so on.

JUNIOR OPERA During a designated period of time, have your kids sing everything they want to say.

THE QUIET GAME Need a good giggle—or a moment of calm to figure out your route? The driver sets a time limit and everybody must be silent. The last person to make a sound wins.

PLAY WHILE YOU WAIT

NOT THE GOOFY GAME   Have one child name a category. (Some ideas: first names, last names, animals, countries, friends, feelings, foods, hot or cold things, clothing.) Then take turns naming things that fall into that category. You're out if you name something that doesn't belong in the category—or if you can't think of another item to name. When only one person remains, start again. Choose categories depending on where you're going or where you've been— historic topics if you've seen a historic sight, animal topics before or after the zoo, upside-down things if you've been to the circus, and so on. Make the game harder by choosing category items in A-B-C order.

DRUTHERS How do your kids really feel about things? Just ask. "Would you rather eat worms or hamburgers? Hamburgers or candy?" Choose serious and silly topics—and have fun!

BUILD A STORY "Once upon a time there lived . . ." Finish the sentence and ask the rest of your family, one at a time, to add another sentence or two. Bring a tape recorder along to record the narrative—and you can enjoy your creation again and again.

CLASSIC GAMES

"I SEE SOMETHING YOU DON'T SEE, AND IT IS BLUE." Stuck for a way to get your youngsters to settle down in a museum? Sit them down on a bench in the middle of a room and play this vintage favorite. The leader gives just one clue—the color—and everybody guesses away.

"I'M GOING TO THE GROCERY..." The first player begins, "I'm going to the grocery and I'm going to buy . . ." and finishes the sentence with the name of an object that begins with the letter "A" and is found in grocery stores. The second player repeats what the first player has said, and adds the name of another item that starts with "B." The third player repeats everything that has been said so far and adds something that begins with "C" and so on through the alphabet. Anyone who skips or misremembers an item is out (or decide up front that you'll give hints to all who need 'em). You can modify the theme depending on where you're going that day, as "I'm going to X and I'm going to see . . ."

FAMILY ARK Noah had his ark—here's your chance to build your own. It's easy. Just start naming animals and work your way through the alphabet, from antelope to zebra.